Amphitryon, or The Two Sosias by John Dryden

A Comedy

John Dryden was born on August 9th, 1631 in the village rectory of Aldwincle near Thrapston in Northamptonshire. As a boy Dryden lived in the nearby village of Titchmarsh, Northamptonshire. In 1644 he was sent to Westminster School as a King's Scholar.

Dryden obtained his BA in 1654, graduating top of the list for Trinity College, Cambridge that year.

Returning to London during The Protectorate, Dryden now obtained work with Cromwell's Secretary of State, John Thurloe.

At Cromwell's funeral on 23 November 1658 Dryden was in the company of the Puritan poets John Milton and Andrew Marvell. The setting was to be a sea change in English history. From Republic to Monarchy and from one set of lauded poets to what would soon become the Age of Dryden.

The start began later that year when Dryden published the first of his great poems, Heroic Stanzas (1658), a eulogy on Cromwell's death.

With the Restoration of the Monarchy in 1660 Dryden celebrated in verse with Astraea Redux, an authentic royalist panegyric.

With the re-opening of the theatres after the Puritan ban, Dryden began to also write plays. His first play, The Wild Gallant, appeared in 1663 but was not successful. From 1668 on he was contracted to produce three plays a year for the King's Company, in which he became a shareholder. During the 1660s and '70s, theatrical writing was his main source of income.

In 1667, he published Annus Mirabilis, a lengthy historical poem which described the English defeat of the Dutch naval fleet and the Great Fire of London in 1666. It established him as the pre-eminent poet of his generation, and was crucial in his attaining the posts of Poet Laureate (1668) and then historiographer royal (1670).

This was truly the Age of Dryden, he was the foremost English Literary figure in Poetry, Plays, translations and other forms.

In 1694 he began work on what would be his most ambitious and defining work as translator, The Works of Virgil (1697), which was published by subscription. It was a national event.

John Dryden died on May 12th, 1700, and was initially buried in St. Anne's cemetery in Soho, before being exhumed and reburied in Westminster Abbey ten days later.

Index of Contents
A SHORT HISTORY OF THE PLAY
INTRODUCTION AND PROLOGUE
TO THE HONOURABLE SIR WILLIAM LEVESON GOWER, BARONET
PROLOGUE - SPOKEN BY MRS BRACEGIRDLE
DRAMATIS PERSONÆ
SCENE—Thebes

ACT I
SCENE I
SCENE II—Amphitryon's Palace.
ACT II
SCENE I—A Night Scene of a Palace
SCENE II
ACT III
SCENE I—Before Amphitryon's Palace
ACT IV
SCENE I
ACT V
SCENE I
EPILOGUE - SPOKEN BY PHÆDRA
John Dryden – A Short Biography
John Dryden – A Concise Bibliography

A SHORT HISTORY OF THE PLAY

John Dryden wrote this play in 1690. The work here is the one edited by Sir Walter Scott in 1808.

Egregiam verò laudem, et spolia ampla refertis,
Una dolo Divûm si fæmina victa duorum est.—Virgil

This work by Dryden is based on Molière's 1668 play of the same name which was in turn based on the story of the Greek mythological character Amphitryon as told by Plautus in his play from ca. 190-185 B.C. Dryden's play, which focuses on themes of sexual morality and power, premiered in London in 1690. Notable innovations in Dryden's adaptation compared to previous plays on Amphitryon included music by Henry Purcell and the character of Phaedra, who flirts with Sosia but is eventually won over by Mercury's promises of wealth.

Although popular with the public, Dryden's play was attacked by Jeremy Collier in his 1698 pamphlet entitled "A Short View of the Immortality of the Stage" for undermining social mores and attacking the political values of his day. The work was later altered significantly by John Hawkesworth for a production in 1756, with him removing what he considered the morally objectionable material.

INTRODUCTION AND PROLOGUE

Plautus, the venerable father of Roman comedy, who flourished during the second Punic war, left us a play on the subject of Amphitryon, which has had the honour to be deemed worthy of imitation by Moliere and Dryden. It cannot be expected, that the plain, blunt, and inartificial stile of so rude an age should bear any comparison with that of authors who enjoyed the highest advantages of the polished times, to which they were an ornament. But the merit of having devised and embodied most of the comic distresses, which have excited laughter throughout so many ages, is to be attributed to the ancient bard, upon whose original conception of the plot his successors have made few and inconsiderable improvements. It is true, that, instead of a formal Prologus, who stepped forth, in the character of Mercury, and gravely detailed to the audience the plot of the play, Moliere and Dryden have introduced it in the modern more artificial method, by the dialogue of the actors in the first scene. It is true, also, that with great contempt of one of the unities, afterwards deemed so indispensible by the ancients, Plautus introduces the birth of Hercules into a play, founded upon the intrigue which occasioned that event. Yet with all these disadvantages, and that of the rude flatness of his dialogue,—resting frequently, for wit, upon the most miserable puns,—the comic device of the two Sosias; the errors into which the malice of Mercury plunges his unlucky original; the quarrel of Alcmena with her real husband, and her reconciliation with Jupiter in his stead; the final confronting of the two Amphitryos; and the astonishment of the unfortunate general, at finding every proof of his identity exhibited by his rival,—are all, however rudely sketched, the inventions of the Roman poet. In one respect it would seem, that the jeu de theatre, necessary to render the piece probable upon the stage, was better managed in the time of Plautus than in that of Dryden and Moliere. Upon a modern stage it is evidently difficult to introduce two pair of characters, so extremely alike as to make it at all probable, or even possible, that the mistakes, depending upon their extreme resemblance, could take place. But, favoured by the masks and costume of the ancient theatre, Plautus contrived to render Jupiter and Mercury so exactly like Amphitryon and Sosia, that they were obliged to retain certain marks, supposed to be invisible to the other persons of the drama, by which the audience themselves might be enabled to distinguish the gods from the mortals, whose forms they had assumed.

The modern poets have treated the subject, which they had from Plautus, each according to the fashion of his country; and so far did the correctness of the French stage exceed ours at that period, that the palm of the comic writing must be, at once, awarded to Moliere. For, though Dryden had the advantage of the French author's labours, from which, and from Plautus, he has translated liberally, the wretched taste of the age has induced him to lard the piece with gratuitous indelicacy. He is, in general, coarse and vulgar, where Moliere is witty; and where the Frenchman ventures upon a double meaning, the Englishman always contrives to make it a single one. Yet although inferior to Moliere, and accommodated to the gross taste of the seventeenth century, "Amphitryon" is one of the happiest effusions of Dryden's comic muse. He has enriched the plot by the intrigue of Mercury and Phædra; and the petulant interested "Queen of Gipsies," as her lover terms her, is no bad paramour for the God of Thieves.

In the scenes of a higher cast, Dryden far outstrips both the French and Roman poet. The sensation to be expressed is not that of sentimental affection, which the good father of Olympus was not capable of feeling; but love, of that grosser and subordinate kind which prompted Jupiter in his intrigues, has been by none of the ancient poets expressed in more beautiful verse than that in which Dryden has clothed it, in the scenes between Jupiter and Alcmena. Even Milbourne, who afterwards attacked our author with such malignant asperity, was so sensible of the merit of "Amphitryon," that he addressed to the publisher the following letter and copy of verses, which Mr Malone's industry recovered from among Mr Tonson's papers.

"Mr Tonson, Yarmouth, November 24th—90.

"You'l wonder perhaps at this from a stranger; but ye reason of it may perhaps abate somewhat of ye miracle, and it's this. On Thursday the twentyth instant, I receiv'd Mr Drydens Amphytrio: I leave out the Greeke termination, as not so proper in my opinion, in English. But to passe that; I liked the play, and read it over with as much of criticisme and ill nature as ye time (being about one in ye morning, and in bed,) would permit. Going to sleep very well pleasd, I could not leave my bed in ye morning without this sacrifice to the authours genius: it was too sudden to be correct, but it was very honestly meant, and is submitted to yours and Mr Ds. disposall.

"Hail, Prince of Witts! thy fumbling Age is past,
Thy youth and witt and art's renewed at last.

So on some rock the Joviall bird assays
Her ore-grown beake, that marke of age, to rayse;
That done, through yield'ing air she cutts her way,
And strongly stoops againe, and breaks the trembling prey.
What though prodigious thunder stripp'd thy brows
Of envy'd bays, and the dull world allows
Shadwell should wear them,—wee'll applaud the change;
Where nations feel it, who can think it strange!
So have I seen the long-ear'd brute aspire
To drest commode with every smallest wire;
With nightrail hung on shoulders, gravely stalke,
Like bawd attendant on Aurelias walke.
Hang't! give the fop ingratefull world its will;
He wears the laurel,—thou deservs't it still.
Still smooth, as when, adorn'd with youthful pride,
For thy dear sake the blushing virgins dyed;
When the kind gods of witt and love combined,
And with large gifts thy yielding soul refined.
"Not Phœbus could with gentler words pursue
His flying Daphne, not the morning dew
Falls softer than the words of amorous Jove,
When melting, dying, for Alcmene's love.
"Yet briske and airy too, thou fill'st the stage,
Unbroke by fortune, undecayed by age.
French wordy witt by thine was long surpast;
Now Rome's thy captive, and by thee wee taste
Of their rich dayntyes; but so finely drest,
Theirs was a country meal, thine a triumphant feast.
"If this to thy necessityes wee ow,
O, may they greater still and greater grow!
Nor blame the wish; Plautus could write in chaines,
Wee'll blesse thy wants, while wee enjoy thy pains.
Wealth makes the poet lazy, nor can fame,
That gay attendant of a spritely flame,
A Dorset or a Wycherly invite,
Because they feel no pinching wants, to write.

"Go on! endenizon the Romane slave;
Let an eternal spring adorne his grave;
His ghost would gladly all his fame submitt
To thy strong judgment and thy piercing witt.
Purged by thy hand, he speaks immortall sense,
And pleases all with modish excellence.
Nor would we have thee live on empty praise
The while, for, though we cann't restore the bays,
While thou writ'st thus,—to pay thy merites due,
Wee'll give the claret and the pension too."

Milbourne concludes, by desiring to be supplied with such of our author's writings, as he had not already, to be sent to Yarmouth in Norfolk, where he probably had then a living.

"Amphitryon" was produced in the same year with "Don Sebastian;" and although it cannot be called altogether an original performance, yet it contains so much original writing as to shew, that our author's vein of poetry was, in his advanced age, distinguished by the same rapid fluency, as when he first began to write for the stage.

This comedy was acted and printed in 1690. It was very favourably received; and continued long to be what is called a stock-play.

TO THE HONOURABLE SIR WILLIAM LEVESON GOWER, BARONET

There is one kind of virtue which is inborn in the nobility, and indeed in most of the ancient families of this nation; they are not apt to insult on the misfortunes of their countrymen. But you, sir, I may tell it without flattery, have grafted on this natural commiseration, and raised it to a nobler virtue. As you have been pleased to honour me, for a long time, with some part of your esteem, and your good will; so, in particular, since the late Revolution, you have increased the proofs of your kindness to me; and not suffered the difference of opinions, which produce such hatred and enmity in the brutal part of human kind, to remove you from the settled basis of your good nature, and good sense. This nobleness of yours, had it been exercised on an enemy, had certainly been a point of honour, and as such I might have justly recommended it to the world; but that of constancy to your former choice, and the pursuance of your first favours, are virtues not over-common amongst Englishmen. All things of honour have, at best, somewhat of ostentation in them, and self-love; there is a pride of doing more than is expected from us, and more than others would have done. But to proceed in the same track of goodness, favour, and protection, is to shew that a man is acted by a thorough principle: it carries somewhat of tenderness in it, which is humanity in a heroical degree; it is a kind of unmoveable good-nature; a word which is commonly despised, because it is so seldom practised. But, after all, it is the most generous virtue, opposed to the most degenerate vice, which is that of ruggedness and harshness to our fellow-creatures.

It is upon this knowledge of you, sir, that I have chosen you, with your permission, to be the patron of this poem. And as, since this wonderful Revolution, I have begun with the best pattern of humanity, the Earl of Leicester, I shall continue to follow the same method, in all to whom I shall address; and endeavour to pitch on such only, as have been pleased to own me, in this ruin of my small fortune; who, though they are of a contrary opinion themselves, yet blame not me for adhering to a lost cause; and judging for myself, what I cannot chuse but judge, so long as I am a patient sufferer, and no disturber of the government. Which, if it be a severe penance, as a great wit has told the world, it is at least enjoined me by myself: and Sancho Pança, as much fool as I, was observed to discipline his body no farther than he found he could endure the smart.

You see, sir, I am not entertaining you like Ovid, with a lamentable epistle from Pontus: I suffer no more than I can easily undergo; and so long as I enjoy my liberty, which is the birth-right of an Englishman, the rest shall never go near my heart. The merry philosopher is more to my humour than the melancholic; and I find no disposition in myself to cry, while the mad world is daily supplying me with such occasions of laughter. The more reasonable sort of my countrymen have shewn so much favour to this piece, that they give me no doubt of their protection for the future.

As you, sir, have been pleased to follow the example of their goodness, in favouring me; so give me leave to say that I follow yours, in this dedication to a person of a different persuasion. Though I must confess withal, that I have had a former encouragement from you for this address; and the warm remembrance of your noble hospitality to me, at Trentham, when some years ago I visited my friends and relations in your country, has ever since given me a violent temptation to this boldness.

It is true, were this comedy wholly mine, I should call it a trifle, and perhaps not think it worth your patronage; but, when the names of Plautus and Moliere are joined in it, that is, the two greatest names of ancient and modern comedy, I must not presume so far on their reputation, to think their best and most unquestioned productions can be termed little. I will not give you the trouble of acquainting you what I have added, or altered, in either of them, so much, it may be, for the worse; but only, that the difference of our stage, from the Roman and the French, did so require it. But I am afraid, for my own interest, the world will too easily discover, that more than half of it is mine; and that the rest is rather a lame imitation of their excellencies, than a just translation. It is enough, that the reader know by you, that I neither deserve nor desire any applause from it: if I have performed anything, it is the genius of my authors that inspired me; and, if it pleased in representation let the actors share the praise amongst themselves. As for Plautus and Moliere, they are dangerous people; and I am too weak a gamester to put myself into their form of play. But what has been wanting on my part, has been abundantly supplied by the excellent composition of Mr Purcell; in whose person we have at length found an Englishman, equal with the best abroad. At least, my opinion of him has been such, since his happy and judicious performances in the late opera, and the experience I have had of him, in the setting my three songs for this "Amphitryon:" to all which, and particularly to the composition of the pastoral dialogue, the numerous choir of fair ladies gave so just an applause on the third day. I am only sorry, for my own sake, that there was one star wanting, as beautiful as any in our hemisphere; that young Berenice, who is misemploying all her charms on stupid country souls, that can never know the value of them; and losing the triumphs, which are ready prepared for her, in the court and town. And yet I know not whether I am so much a loser by her absence; for I have reason to apprehend the sharpness of her judgment, if it were not allayed with the sweetness of her nature; and, after all, I fear she may come time enough to discover a thousand imperfections in my play, which might have passed on vulgar understandings. Be pleased to use the authority of a father over her, on my behalf: enjoin her to keep her own thoughts of "Amphitryon" to herself; or at least not to compare him too strictly with Moliere's. It is true, I have an interest in this partiality of hers: but withal, I plead some sort of merit for it, in being so particularly, as I am,

SIR,

Your most obedient,
Humble servant,
JOHN DRYDEN.

October 24th, 1690.

PROLOGUE

SPOKEN BY MRS BRACEGIRDLE

The labouring bee, when his sharp sting is gone,
Forgets his golden work, and turns a drone:
Such is a satire, when you take away
That rage, in which his noble vigour lay.
What gain you, by not suffering him to teaze ye?
He neither can offend you now, nor please ye.

The honey-bag, and venom, lay so near,
That both together you resolved to tear;
And lost your pleasure, to secure your fear.
How can he show his manhood, if you bind him
To box, like boys, with one hand tied behind him?
This is plain levelling of wit; in which
The poor has all the advantage, not the rich.
The blockhead stands excused, for wanting sense;
And wits turn blockheads in their own defence.
Yet, though the stage's traffic is undone,
Still Julian's interloping trade goes on:
Though satire on the theatre you smother,
Yet, in lampoons, you libel one another.
The first produces, still, a second jig;
You whip them out, like school-boys, till they gig;
And with the same success, our readers guess,
For every one still dwindles to a less;
And much good malice is so meanly drest,
That we would laugh, but cannot find the jest.

If no advice your rhyming rage can stay,
Let not the ladies suffer in the fray:
Their tender sex is privileged from war;
'Tis not like knights, to draw upon the fair.
What fame expect you from so mean a prize?
We wear no murdering weapons, but our eyes.

Our sex, you know, was after yours designed;
The last perfection of the Maker's mind:
Heaven drew out all the gold for us, and left your dross behind.
Beauty, for valour's best reward, he chose;
Peace, after war; and, after toil, repose.

Hence, ye profane, excluded from our sights;
And, charmed by day with honour's vain delights,
Go, make your best of solitary nights.
Recant betimes, 'tis prudence to submit;
Our sex is still your over-match in wit:
We never fail, with new, successful arts,
To make fine fools of you, and all your parts.

DRAMATIS PERSONÆ
Jupiter
Mercury
Phœbus
Amphitryon, the Theban General
Sosia, his Slave
Gripus, a Theban Judge

Polidas,   Officers of the Theban Army
Tranio,
Alcmena, Wife to Amphitryon
Phædra,   Her Slaves
Bromia
Night

SCENE—Thebes

ACT I

SCENE I

Mercury and Phœbus descend in two Machines.

PHŒBUS - Know you the reason of this present summons?
'Tis neither council day, nor is this heaven.
What business has our Jupiter on earth?
Why more at Thebes than any other place?
And why we two, of all the herd of gods,
Are chosen out to meet him in consult?
They call me God of Wisdom;
But Mars and Vulcan, the two fools of heaven,
Whose wit lies in their anvil and their sword,
Know full as much as I.

MERCURY - And Venus may know more than both of us;
For 'tis some petticoat affair, I guess.

I have discharged my duty, which was, to summon you, Phœbus: we shall know more anon, when the Thunderer comes down. 'Tis our part to obey our father; for, to confess the truth, we two are little better than sons of harlots; and, if Jupiter had not been pleased to take a little pains with our mothers, instead of being gods, we might have been a couple of link-boys.

PHŒBUS - But know you nothing farther, Hermes? What news in court?

MERCURY - There has been a devilish quarrel, I can tell you, between Jupiter and Juno. She threatened to sue him in the spiritual court for some matrimonial omissions; and he stood upon his prerogative: then she hit him in the teeth of all his bastards; and your name and mine were used with less reverence than became our godships. They were both in their cups; and at last the matter grew so high, that they were ready to have thrown stars at one another's heads.

PHŒBUS - 'Twas happy for me that I was at my vocation, driving day-light about the world. But I had rather stand my father's thunderbolts, than my stepmother's railing.

MERCURY - When the tongue-battle was over, and the championess had harnessed her peacocks to go for Samos, and hear the prayers that were made to her—

PHŒBUS - By the way, her worshippers had a bad time on't; she was in a damnable humour for receiving petitions.

MERCURY - Jupiter immediately beckons me aside, and charges me, that, as soon as ever you had set up your horses, you and I should meet him here at Thebes: Now, putting the premises together, as dark as it is, methinks I begin to see day-light.

PHŒBUS - As plain as one of my own beams; she has made him uneasy at home, and he is going to seek his diversion abroad. I see heaven itself is no privileged place for happiness, if a man must carry his wife along with him.

MERCURY - 'Tis neither better nor worse, upon my conscience. He is weary of hunting in the spacious forest of a wife, and is following his game incognito in some little purlieu here at Thebes: that's many an honest man's case on earth too, Jove help them! as indeed he does, to make them cuckolds.

PHŒBUS - But, if so, Mercury, then I, who am a poet, must indite his love-letter; and you, who are by trade a porter, must convey it.

MERCURY - No more; he's coming down souse upon us, and hears as far as he can see too. He's plaguy hot upon the business, I know it by his hard driving.

Jupiter descends.

JUPITER - What, you are descanting upon my actions!
Much good may do you with your politics:
All subjects will be censuring their kings.
Well, I confess I am in love; what then?

PHŒBUS - Some mortal, we presume, of Cadmus' blood;
Some Theban beauty; some new Semele;
Or some Europa.

MERCURY - I'll say that for my father, he's constant to a handsome family; he knows when they have a good smack with them, and snuff's up incense so savourily when 'tis offered by a fair hand,——

JUPITER - Well, my familiar sons, this saucy carriage
I have deserved; for he, who trusts a secret,
Makes his own man his master.
I read your thoughts;
Therefore you may as safely speak as think.

MERCURY - Mine was a very homely thought.—I was considering into what form your almightyship would be pleased to transform yourself to-night: whether you would fornicate in the shape of a bull, or a ram, or an eagle, or a swan; what bird or beast you would please to honour, by transgressing your own laws in his likeness; or, in short, whether you would recreate yourself in feathers, or in leather?

PHŒBUS - Any disguise to hide the king of gods.

JUPITER - I know your malice, Phœbus; you would say,
That, when a monarch sins, it should be secret,
To keep exterior shew of sanctity,
Maintain respect, and cover bad example:
For kings and priests are in a manner bound,
For reverence sake, to be close hypocrites.

PHŒBUS - But what necessitates you to this love,
Which you confess a crime, and yet commit?
For, to be secret makes not sin the less;
'Tis only hidden from the vulgar view;
Maintains, indeed, the reverence due to princes,
But not absolves the conscience from the crime.

JUPITER - I love, because 'twas in the fates I should.

PHŒBUS - With reverence be it spoke, a bad excuse:
Thus every wicked act, in heaven or earth,
May make the same defence. But what is fate?
Is it a blind contingence of events,
Or sure necessity of causes linked,
That must produce effects? Or is't a power,
That orders all things by superior will,
Foresees his work, and works in that foresight?

JUPITER - Fate is, what I,
By virtue of omnipotence, have made it;
And power omnipotent can do no wrong:
Not to myself, because I will it so;
Nor yet to men, for what they are is mine.—
This night I will enjoy Amphitryon's wife;
For, when I made her, I decreed her such
As I should please to love. I wrong not him
Whose wife she is; for I reserved my right,
To have her while she pleased me; that once past,
She shall be his again.

MERCURY - Here's omnipotence with a vengeance! to make a man a cuckold, and yet not to do him wrong! Then I find, father Jupiter, that when you made fate, you had the wit to contrive a holiday for yourself now and then; for you kings never enact a law, but you have a kind of an eye to your own prerogative.

PHŒBUS - If there be no such thing as right and wrong
Of an eternal being, I have done;
But if there be,——

JUPITER - Peace, thou disputing fool!—
Learn this; If thou could'st comprehend my ways,
Then thou wert Jove, not I; yet thus far know,
That, for the good of human kind, this night
I shall beget a future Hercules,

Who shall redress the wrongs of injured mortals,
Shall conquer monsters, and reform the world.

MERCURY - Ay, brother Phœbus; and our father made all those monsters for Hercules to conquer, and contrived all those vices on purpose for him to reform too, there's the jest on't.

PHŒBUS - Since arbitrary power will hear no reason,
'Tis wisdom to be silent.

MERCURY - Why that's the point; this same arbitrary power is a knock-down argument; 'tis but a word and a blow. Now methinks, our father speaks out like an honest bare-faced god, as he is; he lays the stress in the right place, upon absolute dominion: I confess, if he had been a man, he might have been a tyrant, if his subjects durst have called him to account. But you, brother Phœbus, are but a mere country gentleman, that never comes to court; that are abroad all day on horseback, making visits about the world; are drinking all night; and, in your cups are still railing at the government. O, these patriots, these bumpkin patriots, are a very silly sort of animal!

JUPITER - My present purpose and design you heard,
To enjoy Amphitryon's wife, the fair Alcmena:
You two must be subservient to my love.

MERCURY - [To Phœbus.] No more of your grumbletonian morals, brother; there's preferment coming; be advised, and pimp dutifully.

JUPITER - Amphitryon, the brave Theban general,
Has overcome his country's foes in fight,
And, in a single duel, slain their king:
His conquering troops are eager on their march
Returning home; while their young general,
More eager to review his beauteous wife,
Posts on before, winged with impetuous love,
And, by to-morrow's dawn, will reach this town.

MERCURY - That's but short warning, father Jupiter; having made no former advances of courtship to her, you have need of your omnipotence, and all your godship, if you mean to be beforehand with him.

PHŒBUS - Then how are we to be employed this evening?
Time's precious, and these summer nights are short;
I must be early up to light the world.

JUPITER - You shall not rise; there shall be no to-morrow.

MERCURY - Then the world's to be at an end, I find.

PHŒBUS - Or else a gap in nature of a day.

JUPITER - A day will be well lost to busy man;
Night shall continue sleep, and care shall cease.
So, many men shall live, and live in peace,
Whom sunshine had betrayed to envious sight,

And sight to sudden rage, and rage to death.
Now, I will have a night for love and me;
A long luxurious night, fit for a god
To quench and empty his immortal heat.

MERCURY - I'll lay on the woman's side for all that, that she shall love longest to-night, in spite of your omnipotence.

PHŒBUS - I shall be cursed by all the labouring trades,
That early rise; but you must be obeyed.

JUPITER - No matter for the cheating part of man,
They have a day's sin less to answer for.

PHŒBUS - When would you have me wake?

JUPITER - Why, when Jove goes to sleep; when I have finished,
Your brother Mercury shall bring you word.—

[Exit Phœbus in his chariot.
Now, Hermes, I must take Amphitryon's form,
To enjoy his wife:
Thou must be Sosia, this Amphitryon's slave;
Who, all this night, is travelling to Thebes,
To tell Alcmena of her lord's approach,
And bring her joyful news of victory.

MERCURY - But why must I be Sosia?

JUPITER - Dull god of wit, thou statue of thyself!
Thou must be Sosia, to keep out Sosia;
Who, by his entrance, might discover Jove,
Disturb my pleasures, raise unruly noise,
And so distract Alcmena's tender soul,
She would not meet my warmth, when I dissolve
Into her lap, nor give down half her love.

MERCURY - Let me alone, I'll cudgel him away;
But I abhor so villainous a shape.

JUPITER - Take it, I charge thee on thy duty, take it;
Nor dare to lay it down, till I command.
I cannot bear a moment's loss of joy.—
Night appears above in a chariot.
Look up, the Night is in her silent chariot,
And rolling just o'er Thebes: Bid her drive slowly,
Or make a double turn about the world;
While I drop Jove, and take Amphitryon's dress,
To be the greater, while I seem the less.

[Exit JUPITER.

MERCURY - [To Night.] Madam Night, a good even to you! Fair and softly, I beseech you, madam; I have a word or two to you from no less a god than Jupiter.

NIGHT - O my nimble-fingered god of theft, what makes you here on earth at this unseasonable hour? What banker's shop is to be broke open to-night? or what clippers, and coiners, and conspirators, have been invoking your deity for their assistance?

MERCURY - Faith, none of those enormities, and yet I am still in my vocation; for you know I am a jack of all trades. At a word, Jupiter is indulging his genius to-night with a certain noble sort of recreation; called wenching; the truth on't is, adultery is its proper name.

NIGHT - Jupiter would do well to stick to his wife, Juno.

MERCURY - He has been married to her above these hundred years; and that's long enough, in conscience, to stick to one woman.

NIGHT - She's his sister too, as well as his wife; that's a double tie of affection to her.

MERCURY - Nay, if he made bold with his own flesh and blood, 'tis likely he will not spare his neighbours.

NIGHT - If I were his wife, I would raise a rebellion against him, for the violation of my bed.

MERCURY - Thou art mistaken, old Night; his wife could raise no faction. All the deities in heaven would take the part of the cuckold-making god, for they are all given to the flesh most damnably. Nay, the very goddesses would stickle in the cause of love; 'tis the way to be popular, to whore and love. For what dost thou think old Saturn was deposed, but that he was cold and impotent, and made no court to the fair ladies? Pallas and Juno themselves, as chaste as they are, cried, Shame on him!—I say unto thee, old Night, woe be to the monarch that has not the women on his side!

NIGHT - Then, by your rule, Mercury, a king who would live happily, must debauch his whole nation of women.

MERCURY - As far as his ready money will go, I mean; for Jupiter himself can't please all of them.— But this is beside my present commission: He has sent me to will and require you to make a swinging long night for him, for he hates to be stinted in his pleasures.

NIGHT - Tell him plainly, I'll rather lay down my commission. What, would he make a bawd of me?

MERCURY - Poor ignorant! why he meant thee for a bawd, when he first made thee. What art thou good for, but to be a bawd? Is not day-light better for mankind, I mean as to any other use, but only for love and fornication? Thou hast been a bawd too, a reverend, primitive, original bawd, from the first hour of thy creation; and all the laudable actions of love have been committed under thy mantle. Pr'ythee, for what dost thou think that thou art worshipped?

NIGHT - Why, for my stars and moonshine.

MERCURY - That is, for holding a candle to iniquity. But if they were put out, thou would'st be doubly worshipped by the willing bashful virgins.

NIGHT - Then, for my quiet, and the sweetness of my sleep.

MERCURY - No:—For thy sweet waking all the night; for sleep comes not upon lovers, till thou art vanished.

NIGHT - But it will be against nature, to make a long winter's night at midsummer.

MERCURY - Trouble not yourself for that: Phœbus is ordered to make a short summer's day to-morrow; so, in four-and-twenty hours, all will be at rights again.

NIGHT - Well, I am edified by your discourse; and my comfort is, that, whatever work is made, I see nothing.

MERCURY - About your business then. Put a spoke into your chariot-wheels, and order the seven stars to halt, while I put myself into the habit of a serving-man, and dress up a false Sosia, to wait upon a false Amphitryon.—Good night, Night.

NIGHT - My service to Jupiter.—Farewell, Mercury.

[NIGHT goes backward. Exit MERCURY.

SCENE II—Amphitryon's Palace

Enter ALCMENA.

ALCMENA - Why was I married to the man I love!
For, had he been indifferent to my choice,
Or had been hated, absence had been pleasure;
But now I fear for my Amphitryon's life:
At home, in private, and secure from war,
I am amidst an host of armed foes,
Sustaining all his cares, pierced with his wounds;
And, if he falls,—which, O ye gods avert!—
Am in Amphitryon slain! Would I were there,
And he were here; so might we change our fates;
That he might grieve for me, and I might die for him.

Enter Phædra, running.

PHAEDRA - Good news, good news, madam; O such admirable news, that, if I kept it in a moment, I should burst with it.

ALCMENA - Is it from the army?

PHAEDRA - No matter.

ALCMENA - From Amphitryon?

PHAEDRA - No matter, neither.

ALCMENA - Answer me, I charge thee, if thy good news be any thing relating to my lord; if it be, assure thyself of a reward.

PHAEDRA - Ay, madam, now you say something to the matter: You know the business of a poor waiting-woman, here upon earth, is to be scraping up something against a rainy day, called the day of marriage; everyone in our own vocation:—But what matter is it to me if my lord has routed the enemy, if I get nothing of their spoils?

ALCMENA - Say, is my lord victorious?

PHAEDRA - Why, he is victorious: indeed I prayed devoutly to Jupiter for a victory; by the same token, that you should give me ten pieces of gold if I brought you news of it.

ALCMENA - They are thine, supposing he be safe too.

PHAEDRA - Nay, that's a new bargain, for I vowed to Jupiter, that then you should give me ten pieces more; but I do undertake for my lord's safety, if you will please to discharge his godship Jupiter of the debt, and take it upon you to pay.

ALCMENA - When he returns in safety, Jupiter and I will pay your vow.

PHAEDRA - And I am sure I articled with Jupiter, that, if I brought you news that my lord was upon return, you should grant me one small favour more, that will cost you nothing.

ALCMENA - Make haste, thou torturer; is my Amphitryon upon return?

PHAEDRA - Promise me, that I shall be your bedfellow to-night, as I have been ever since my lord's absence; unless I shall be pleased to release you of your word.

ALCMENA - That's a small request; 'tis granted.

PHAEDRA - But swear by Jupiter.

ALCMENA - But why by Jupiter?

PHAEDRA - Because he's the greatest: I hate to deal with one of your little baffling gods, that can do nothing but by permission; but Jupiter can swinge you off, if you swear by him, and are forsworn.

ALCMENA - I swear by Jupiter.

PHAEDRA - Then—I believe he is victorious, and I know he is safe; for I looked through the key-hole, and saw him knocking at the gate; and I had the conscience to let him cool his heels there.

ALCMENA - And would'st thou not open to him? Oh, thou traitress!

PHAEDRA - No, I was a little wiser: I left Sosia's wife to let him in; for I was resolved to bring the news, and make my pennyworths out of him, as time shall show.

Enter Jupiter, in the shape of Amphitryon, with Sosia's wife, Bromia. He kisses and embraces Alcmena.

JUPITER - O let me live for ever on those lips!
The nectar of the gods to these is tasteless.
I swear, that, were I Jupiter, this night
I would renounce my heaven, to be Amphitryon.

ALCMENA - Then, not to swear beneath Amphitryon's oath,
(Forgive me, Juno, if I am profane,)
I swear, I would be what I am this night,
And be Alcmena, rather than be Juno.

BROMIA - Good my lord, what is become of my poor bedfellow, your man Sosia? you keep such a billing and cooing here, to set one's mouth a watering—what I say, though I am a poor woman, I have a husband as well as my lady; and should be as glad as she, of a little honest recreation.

PHAEDRA - And what have you done with your old friend, and my old sweetheart, Judge Gripus? has he brought me home a crammed purse, that swells with bribes? if he be rich, I will make him welcome like an honourable magistrate; but if he has not had the wit to sell justice, he judges no causes in my court, I warrant him.

ALCMENA - My lord, you tell me nothing of the battle?
Is Thebes victorious, are our foes destroyed?
For, now I find you safe, I should be glad
To hear you were in danger.

JUPITER - [Aside.] A man had need be a god, to stand the fury of three talking women! I think, in my conscience, I made their tongues of thunder.

BROMIA - [Pulling him on one side.] I asked the first question; answer me, my lord.

PHAEDRA - [Pulling him on the other side.] Peace! mine is a lover, and yours but a husband; and my judge is my lord too; the title shall take place, and I will be answered.

JUPITER - Sosia is safe; Gripus is rich; both coming;
I rode before them, with a lover's haste.——
Was e'er poor god so worried? but for my love,
I wish I were in heaven again with Juno. [Aside.

ALCMENA - Then I, it seems, am last to be regarded?

JUPITER - Not so, my love; but these obstreperous tongues
Have snatched their answers first; they will be heard;
And surely Jove would never answer prayer
That woman made, but only to be freed
From their eternal noise. Make haste to bed;
There let me tell my story, in thy arms;
There, in the gentle pauses of our love,
Betwixt our dyings, ere we live again,
Thou shalt be told the battle, and success;
Which I shall oft begin, and then break off;
For love will often interrupt my tale,

And make so sweet confusion in our talk,
That thou shalt ask, and I shall answer things,
That are not of a piece; but patched with kisses,
And sighs, and murmurs, and imperfect speech;
And nonsense shall be eloquent, in love.

BROMIA - [To PHAEDRA.] My lord is very hot upon it: this absence is a great friend to us poor neglected wives; it makes us new again.

ALCMENA - I am the fool of love; and find within me
The fondness of a bride, without the fear.
My whole desires and wishes are in you.

PHAEDRA - [Aside.] My lady's eyes are pinking to bed-ward too: now is she to look very sleepy, counterfeiting yawning,—but she shall ask me leave first.

ALCMENA - Great Juno, thou, whose holy care presides
Over the nuptial bed, pour all thy blessings
On this auspicious night!

JUPITER - Juno may grudge; for she may fear a rival
In those bright eyes; but Jupiter will grant,
And doubly bless this night.

PHAEDRA - [Aside.] But Jupiter should ask my leave
first, were he here in person.

ALCMENA - Bromia, prepare the bed:
The tedious journey has disposed my lord
To seek his needful rest. [Exit Bromia.

PHAEDRA - 'Tis very true, madam; the poor gentleman must needs be weary; and, therefore, it was not ill contrived, that he must lie alone to-night, to recruit himself with sleep, and lay in enough for to-morrow night, when you may keep him waking.

ALCMENA - [To Jupiter.] I must confess, I made a kind of promise.——

PHAEDRA - [Almost crying.] A kind of promise, do you call it? I see you would fain be coming off. I am sure you swore to me, by Jupiter, that I should be your bedfellow; and I'll accuse you to him, too, the first prayers I make; and I'll pray o' purpose, too, that I will, though I have not prayed to him this seven years.

JUPITER - O, the malicious hilding!

ALCMENA - I did swear, indeed, my lord.

JUPITER - Forswear thyself; for Jupiter but laughs
At lovers' perjuries.

PHAEDRA - The more shame for him, if he does: there would be a fine god, indeed, for us women to worship, if he laughs when our sweethearts cheat us of our maidenheads. No, no, Jupiter is an honester gentleman than you make of him.

JUPITER - I'm all on fire; and would not lose this night,
To be the master of the universe.

PHAEDRA - Ay, my lord, I see you are on fire; but the devil a bucket shall be brought to quench it, without my leave. You may go to bed, madam; but you shall see how heaven will bless your night's work, if you forswear yourself:—Some fool, some mere elder-brother, or some blockheadly hero, Jove, I beseech thee, send her!

JUPITER - [Aside.] Now I could call my thunder to revenge me,
But that were to confess myself a god,
And then I lost my love!——Alcmena, come;
By heaven I have a bridegroom's fervour for thee,
As I had ne'er enjoyed.

ALCMENA - She has my oath; [Sighing.
And sure she may release it, if she pleases.

PHAEDRA - Why truly, madam, I am not cruel in my nature, to poor distressed lovers; for it may be my own case another day: and therefore, if my lord pleases to consider me—

JUPITER - Any thing, any thing! but name thy wish, and have it.

PHAEDRA - Ay, now you say, any thing, any thing; but you would tell me another story to-morrow morning. Look you, my lord, here is a hand open to receive; you know the meaning of it; I am for nothing but the ready—

JUPITER - Thou shalt have all the treasury of heaven.

PHAEDRA - Yes, when you are Jupiter, to dispose of it.

JUPITER - [Aside.] I had forgot, and shewed myself a god:
This love can make a fool of Jupiter.

PHAEDRA - You have forgot some part of the enemies' spoil, I warrant you. I see a little trifling diamond upon your finger; and I am proud enough to think it would become mine too.

JUPITER - Here take it.—[Taking a Ring off his Finger, and giving it.
This is a very woman;
Her sex is avarice, and she, in one,
Is all her sex.

PHAEDRA - Ay, ay, 'tis no matter what you say of us. What, would you have your money out of the treasury, without paying the officers their fees? Go, get you together, you naughty couple, till you are both weary of worrying one another; and then to-morrow morning I shall have another fee for parting you.

[PHAEDRA goes out before ALCMENA with a light.

JUPITER - Why now, I am indeed the lord of all;
For what's to be a god, but to enjoy?
Let human kind their sovereign's leisure wait;
Love is, this night, my great affair of state:
Let this one night of providence be void;
All Jove, for once, is on himself employ'd.
Let unregarded altars smoke in vain;
And let my subjects praise me, or complain:
Yet if, betwixt my intervals of bliss,
Some amorous youth his orisons address,
His prayer is in a happy hour preferred;
And when Jove loves, a lover shall be heard.

[Exit.

ACT II

SCENE I—A Night Scene of a Palace

SOSIA, with a Dark-Lanthorn; MERCURY, in Sosia's shape, with a Dark-Lanthorn also.

SOSIA - Was not the devil in my master, to send me out this dreadful dark night, to bring the news of his victory to my lady? and was not I possessed with ten devils, for going on his errand, without a convoy for the safeguard of my person? Lord, how am I melted into sweat with fear! I am diminished of my natural weight, above two stone: I shall not bring half myself home again, to my poor wife and family; I have been in an ague fit, ever since shut of evening; what with the fright of trees by the highway, which looked maliciously, like thieves, by moonshine; and what with bulrushes by the river-side, that shaked like spears and lances at me. Well, the greatest plague of a serving-man, is to be hired to some great lord! They care not what drudgery they put upon us, while they lie lolling at their ease a-bed, and stretch their lazy limbs, in expectation of the whore which we are fetching for them.

MERCURY - [Aside.] He is but a poor mortal, that suffers this; but I, who am a god, am degraded to a foot-pimp; a waiter without doors! a very civil employment for a deity!

SOSIA - The better sort of them will say, "Upon my honour," at every word; yet ask them for our wages, and they plead the privilege of their honour, and will not pay us; nor let us take our privilege of the law upon them. These are a very hopeful sort of patriots, to stand up, as they do, for liberty and property of the subject: There's conscience for you!

MERCURY - [Aside.] This fellow has something of the republican spirit in him.

SOSIA - [Looking about him.] Stay; this, methinks, should be our house; and I should thank the gods now for bringing me safe home: but, I think, I had as good let my devotions alone, till I have got the reward for my good news, and then thank them once for all; for, if I praise them before I am safe within doors, some damned mastiff dog may come out and worry me; and then my thanks are thrown away upon them.

MERCURY - [Aside.] Thou art a wicked rogue, and wilt have thy bargain beforehand; therefore thou get'st not into the house this night; and thank me accordingly as I use thee.

SOSIA - Now am I to give my lady an account of my lord's victory; 'tis good to exercise my parts beforehand, and file my tongue into eloquent expressions, to tickle her ladyship's imagination.

MERCURY - [Aside.] Good! and here's the god of eloquence to judge of thy oration.

SOSIA - [Setting down his Lanthorn.] This lanthorn, for once, shall be my lady; because she is the lamp of all beauty and perfection.

MERCURY - [Aside.] No, rogue! 'tis thy lord is the lanthorn by this time, or Jupiter is turned fumbler.

SOSIA - Then thus I make my addresses to her:—[Bows.] Madam, my lord has chosen me out, as the most faithful, though the most unworthy, of his followers, to bring your ladyship this following account of our glorious expedition. Then she,—O my poor Sosia, [In a shrill tone.] how am I overjoyed to see thee! She can say no less.—Madam, you do me too much honour, and the world will envy me this glory:—Well answered on my side. And how does my lord Amphitryon?—Madam, he always does like a man of courage, when he is called by honour.—There I think I nicked it.—But when will he return?—As soon as possibly he can; but not so soon as his impatient heart could wish him with your ladyship.

MERCURY - [Aside.] When Thebes is an university, thou deservest to be their orator.

SOSIA - But what does he do, and what does he say? Pr'ythee tell me something more of him.—He always says less than he does, madam; and his enemies have found it to their cost.—Where the devil did I learn these elegancies and gallantries!

MERCURY - So, he has all the natural endowments of a fop, and only wants the education.

SOSIA - [Staring up to the sky.] What, is the devil in the night! She's as long as two nights. The seven stars are just where they were seven hours ago! high day—high night, I mean, by my favour. What, has Phœbus been playing the good fellow, and overslept himself, that he forgets his duty to us mortals!

MERCURY - How familiarly the rascal treats us gods! but I shall make him alter his tone immediately.

[MERCURY comes nearer, and stands just before him.

SOSIA - [Seeing him, and starting back, aside.] How now? what, do my eyes dazzle, or is my dark lanthorn false to me! is not that a giant before our door? or a ghost of somebody slain in the late battle? If he be, 'tis unconscionably done, to fright an honest man thus, who never drew weapon wrathfully in all my life. Whatever wight he be, I am devilishly afraid, that's certain; but, 'tis discretion to keep my own counsel; I'll sing, that I may seem valiant.

[SOSIA sings; and, as MERCURY speaks, by little and little drops his voice.

MERCURY - What saucy companion is this, that deafens us with his hoarse voice? What midnight ballad-singer have we here? I shall teach the villain to leave off catterwauling.

SOSIA - I would I had courage, for his sake, that I might teach him to call my singing catterwauling! an illiterate rogue! an enemy to the muses, and to music.

MERCURY - There is an ill savour that offends my nostrils and it wafteth this way.

SOSIA - He has smelt me out; my fear has betrayed me into this savour. I am a dead man: the bloody villain is at his fee, fa, fum, already.

MERCURY - Stand, who goes there?

SOSIA - A friend.

MERCURY - What friend?

SOSIA - Why, a friend to all the world, that will give me leave to live peaceably.

MERCURY - I defy peace and all its works; my arms are out of exercise, they have mauled nobody these three days: I long for an honourable occasion to pound a man, and lay him asleep at the first buffet.

SOSIA - [Aside.] That would almost do me a kindness; for I have been kept waking, without tipping one wink of sleep, these three nights.

MERCURY - Of what quality are you, fellow?

SOSIA - Why, I am a man, fellow.—Courage, Sosia!

MERCURY - What kind of man?

SOSIA - Why, a two-legged man; what man should I be? [Aside.] I must bear up to him, he may prove as arrant a milksop as myself.

MERCURY - Thou art a coward, I warrant thee; do not I hear thy teeth chatter in thy head?

SOSIA - Ay, ay; that's only a sign they would be snapping at thy nose. [Aside.] Bless me, what an arm and fist he has, with great thumbs too; and golls and knuckle-bones of a very butcher!

MERCURY - Sirrah, from whence came you, and whither go you; answer me directly, upon pain of assassination.

SOSIA - I am coming from whence I came, and am going whither I go,—that's directly home; though this is somewhat an uncivil manner of proceeding, at the first sight of a man, let me tell you.

MERCURY - Then, to begin our better acquaintance, let me first make you a small present of this box o' the ear— [Strikes him.

SOSIA - If I were as choleric a fool as you are now, here would be fine work betwixt us two; but I am a little better bred, than to disturb the sleeping neighbourhood; and so good-night, friend— [Is going.

MERCURY - [Stopping him.] Hold, sir; you and I must not part so easily; once more, whither are you going?

SOSIA - Why I am going as fast as I can, to get out of the reach of your clutches. Let me but only knock at the door there.

MERCURY - What business have you at that door, sirrah?

SOSIA - This is our house; and, when I am got in, I will tell you more.

MERCURY - Whose house is this, sauciness, that you are so familiar with, to call it ours?

SOSIA - 'Tis mine, in the first place; and next, my master's; for I lie in the garret, and he lies under me.

MERCURY - Have your master and you no names, sirrah?

SOSIA - His name is Amphitryon; hear that, and tremble.

MERCURY - What, my lord general?

SOSIA - O, has his name mollified you! I have brought you down a peg lower already, friend.

MERCURY - And your name is—

SOSIA - Lord, friend, you are so very troublesome—what should my name be, but Sosia?

MERCURY - How, Sosia, say you? how long have you taken up that name, sirrah?

SOSIA - Here's a fine question! Why I never took it up, friend; it was born with me.

MERCURY - What, was your name born Sosia? take this remembrance for that lie. [Beats him.

SOSIA - Hold, friend! you are so very flippant with your hands, you won't hear reason: What offence has my name done you, that you should beat me for it? S. O. S. I. A. they are as civil, honest, harmless letters, as any are in the whole alphabet.

MERCURY - I have no quarrel to the name; but that 'tis e'en too good for you, and 'tis none of yours.

SOSIA - What, am not I Sosia, say you?

MERCURY - No.

SOSIA - I should think you are somewhat merrily disposed, if you had not beaten me in such sober sadness. You would persuade me out of my heathen name, would you?

MERCURY - Say you are Sosia again, at your peril, sirrah.

SOSIA - I dare say nothing, but thought is free; but whatever I am called, I am Amphitryon's man, and the first letter of my name is S. too. You had best tell me that my master did not send me home to my lady, with news of his victory?

MERCURY - I say, he did not.

SOSIA - Lord, Lord, friend, one of us two is horribly given to lying; but I do not say which of us, to avoid contention.

MERCURY - I say my name is Sosia, and yours is not.

SOSIA - I would you could make good your words; for then I should not be beaten, and you should.

MERCURY - I find you would be Sosia, if you durst; but if I catch you thinking so——

SOSIA - I hope I may think I was Sosia; and I can find no difference between my former self, and my present self, but that I was plain Sosia before, and now I am laced Sosia.

MERCURY - Take this, for being so impudent to think so. [Beats him.

SOSIA - [Kneeling.] Truce a little, I beseech thee! I would be a stock or a stone now by my good will, and would not think at all, for self-preservation. But will you give me leave to argue the matter fairly with you, and promise me to depose that cudgel, if I can prove myself to be that man that I was before I was beaten?

MERCURY - Well, proceed in safety; I promise you I will not beat you.

SOSIA - In the first place, then, is not this town called Thebes?

MERCURY - Undoubtedly.

SOSIA - And is not this house Amphitryon's?

MERCURY - Who denies it?

SOSIA - I thought you would have denied that too; for all hang upon a string. Remember then, that those two preliminary articles are already granted. In the next place, did not the aforesaid Amphitryon beat the Teleboans, kill their king Pterelas, and send a certain servant, meaning somebody, that for sake-sake shall be nameless, to bring a present to his wife, with news of his victory, and of his resolution to return to-morrow?

MERCURY - This is all true, to a very tittle; but who is that certain servant? there's all the question.

SOSIA - Is it peace or war betwixt us?

MERCURY - Peace.

SOSIA - I dare not wholly trust that abominable cudgel; but 'tis a certain friend of yours and mine, that had a certain name before he was beaten out of it; but if you are a man that depend not altogether upon force and brutality, but somewhat also upon reason, now do you bring better proofs, that you are that same certain man; and, in order to it, answer me to certain questions.

MERCURY - I say I am Sosia, Amphitryon's man; what reason have you to urge against it?

SOSIA - What was your father's name?

MERCURY - Davus; who was an honest husbandman, whose sister's name was Harpage, that was married, and died in a foreign country.

SOSIA - So far you are right, I must confess; and your wife's name is—

MERCURY - Bromia, a devilish shrew of her tongue, and a vixen of her hands, that leads me a miserable life; keeps me to hard duty a-bed; and beats me every morning when I have risen from her side, without having first—

SOSIA - I understand you, by many a sorrowful token;—this must be I. [Aside.

MERCURY - I was once taken upon suspicion of burglary, and was whipt through Thebes, and branded for my pains.

SOSIA - Right, me again; but if you are I, as I begin to suspect, that whipping and branding might have been past over in silence, for both our credits. And yet now I think on't, if I am I, (as I am I) he cannot be I. All these circumstances he might have heard; but I will now interrogate him upon some private passages.—What was the present that Amphitryon sent by you or me, no matter which of us, to his wife Alcmena?

MERCURY - A buckle of diamonds, consisting of five large stones.

SOSIA - And where are they now?

MERCURY - In a case, sealed with my master's coat of arms.

SOSIA - This is prodigious, I confess; but yet 'tis nothing, now I think on't; for some false brother may have revealed it to him. [Aside.] But I have another question to ask you, of somewhat that passed only betwixt myself and me;—if you are Sosia, what were you doing in the heat of battle?

MERCURY - What a wise man should, that has respect for his own person. I ran into our tent, and hid myself amongst the baggage.

SOSIA - [Aside.] Such another cutting answer; and I must provide myself of another name.—[To him.] And how did you pass your time in that same tent? You need not answer to every circumstance so exactly now; you must lie a little, that I may think you the more me.

MERCURY - That cunning shall not serve your turn, to circumvent me out of my name: I am for plain naked truth. There stood a hogshead of old wine, which my lord reserved for his own drinking——

SOSIA - [Aside.] O the devil! as sure as death, he must have hid himself in that hogshead, or he could never have known that!

MERCURY - And by that hogshead, upon the ground, there lay the kind inviter and provoker of good drinking—

SOSIA - Nay, now I have caught you; there was neither inviter, nor provoker, for I was all alone.

MERCURY - A lusty gammon of—

SOSIA - [Sighing.] Bacon!—that word has quite made an end of me.—Let me see—this must be I, in spite of me; but let me view him nearer.

[Walks about Mercury with his Dark Lanthorn.

MERCURY - What are you walking about me for, with your dark lanthorn?

SOSIA - No harm, friend; I am only surveying a parcel of earth here, that I find we two are about to bargain for:—He's damnable like me, that's certain. Imprimis, there's the patch upon my nose, with a pox to him. Item, A very foolish face, with a long chin at end on't. Item, One pair of shambling legs, with two splay feet belonging to them; and, summa totallis, from head to foot all my bodily apparel. [To Mercury.] Well, you are Sosia; there's no denying it:—but what am I then? for my mind gives me, I am somebody still, if I knew but who I were.

MERCURY - When I have a mind to be Sosia no more, then thou may'st be Sosia again.

SOSIA - I have but one request more to thee; that, though not as Sosia, yet as a stranger, I may go into that house, and carry a civil message to my lady.

MERCURY - No, sirrah; not being Sosia, you have no message to deliver, nor no lady in this house.

SOSIA - Thou canst not be so barbarous, to let me lie in the streets all night, after such a journey, and such a beating; and therefore I am resolved to knock at the door, in my own defence.

MERCURY - If you come near the door, I recal my word, and break off the truce, and then expect—— [Holds up his Cudgel.

SOSIA - No, the devil take me if I do expect; I have felt too well what sour fruit that crab-tree bears: I'll rather beat it back upon the hoof to my lord Amphitryon, to see if he will acknowledge me for Sosia; if he does not, then I am no longer his slave; there's my freedom dearly purchased with a sore drubbing: if he does acknowledge me, then I am Sosia again. So far 'tis tolerably well: but then I shall have a second drubbing for an unfortunate ambassador, as I am; and that's intolerable. [Exit Sosia.

MERCURY - [Alone.] I have fobbed off his excellency pretty well. Now let him return, and make the best of his credentials. I think, too, I have given Jupiter sufficient time for his consummation.—Oh, he has taken his cue; and here he comes as leisurely, and as lank, as if he had emptied himself of the best part of his almightyship.

SCENE II

Enter JUPITER, leading ALCMENA, followed by PHAEDRA. Pages with Torches before them.

JUPITER - [To the Pages.] Those torches are offensive; stand aloof;
For, though they bless me with thy heavenly sight, [To her.
They may disclose the secret I would hide.
The Thebans must not know I have been here;
Detracting crowds would blame me, that I robbed
These happy moments from my public charge,

To consecrate to thy desired embrace;
And I could wish no witness but thyself,
For thou thyself art all I wish to please.

ALCMENA - So long an absence, and so short a stay!
What, but one night! one night of joy and love
Could only pay one night of cares and fears,
And all the rest are an uncancelled sum!—
Curse on this honour, and this public fame;
Would you had less of both, and more of love!

JUPITER - Alcmena, I must go.

ALCMENA - Not yet, my lord.

JUPITER - Indeed I must.

ALCMENA - Indeed you shall not go.

JUPITER - Behold the ruddy streaks o'er yonder hill;
Those are the blushes of the breaking morn,
That kindle day-light to this nether world.

ALCMENA - No matter for the day; it was but made
To number out the hours of busy men.
Let them be busy still, and still be wretched,
And take their fill of anxious drudging day;
But you and I will draw our curtains close,
Extinguish day-light, and put out the sun.
Come back, my lord; in faith you shall retire;
You have not yet lain long enough in bed,
To warm your widowed side.

PHAEDRA - [Aside.] I find my lord is an excellent school-master, my lady is so willing to repeat her lesson.

MERCURY - [Aside.] That's a plaguy little devil; what a roguish eye she has! I begin to like her strangely. She's the perquisite of my place too; for my lady's waiting-woman is the proper fees of my lord's chief gentleman. I have the privilege of a god too; I can view her naked through all her clothes. Let me see, let me see;—I have discovered something, that pleases me already.

JUPITER - Let me not live, but thou art all enjoyment!
So charming and so sweet,
That not a night, but whole eternity,
Were well employed,
To love thy each perfection as it ought.

ALCMENA - [Kissing him.] I'll bribe you with this kiss, to stay a while.

JUPITER - [Kissing her.] A bribe indeed that soon will bring me back;
But, to be just, I must restore your bribe.

How I could dwell for ever on those lips!
O, I could kiss them pale with eagerness!
So soft, by heaven! and such a juicy sweet,
That ripened peaches have not half the flavour.

ALCMENA - Ye niggard gods! you make our lives too long;
You fill them with diseases, wants, and woes,
And only dash them with a little love,
Sprinkled by fits, and with a sparing hand:
Count all our joys, from childhood even to age,
They would but make a day of every year.
Take back your seventy years, the stint of life,
Or else be kind, and cram the quintessence
Of seventy years into sweet seventy days;
For all the rest is flat, insipid being.

JUPITER - But yet one scruple pains me at my parting:
I love so nicely, that I cannot bear
To owe the sweets of love, which I have tasted,
To the submissive duty of a wife.
Tell me, and sooth my passion ere I go,
That, in the kindest moments of the night,
When you gave up yourself to love and me,
You thought not of a husband, but a lover?

ALCMENA - But tell me first, why you would raise a blush
Upon my cheeks, by asking such a question?

JUPITER - I would owe nothing to a name so dull
As husband is, but to a lover all.

ALCMENA - You should have asked me then, when love and night,
And privacy, had favoured your demand.

JUPITER - I ask it now, because my tenderness
Surpasses that of husbands for their wives.
O that you loved like me! then you would find
A thousand, thousand niceties in love.
The common love of sex to sex is brutal;
But love refined will fancy to itself
Millions of gentle cares, and sweet disquiets;
The being happy is not half the joy;
The manner of their happiness is all.
In me, my charming mistress, you behold
A lover that disdains a lawful title,
Such as of monarchs to successive thrones;
The generous lover holds by force of arms,
And claims his crown by conquest.

ALCMENA - Methinks you should be pleased; I give you all
A virtuous and modest wife can give.

JUPITER - No, no; that very name of wife and marriage
Is poison to the dearest sweets of love;
To please my niceness, you must separate
The lover from his mortal foe—the husband.
Give to the yawning husband your cold virtue;
But all your vigorous warmth, your melting sighs,
Your amorous murmurs, be your lover's part.

ALCMENA - I comprehend not what you mean, my lord;
But only love me still, and love me thus,
And think me such as best may please your thought.

JUPITER - There's mystery of love in all I say.—
Farewell; and when you see your husband next,
Think of your lover then.

[Exeunt JUPITER and ALCMENA severally; PHAEDRA - follows her.

MERCURY - [Alone.] Now I should follow him; but love has laid a lime-twig for me, and made a lame god of me. Yet why should I love this Phædra? She's interested, and a jilt into the bargain. Three thousand years hence, there will be a whole nation of such women, in a certain country, that will be called France; and there's a neighbour island, too, where the men of that country will be all interest. O what a precious generation will that be, which the men of the island shall propagate out of the women of the continent!

PHAEDRA re-enters.

And so much for prophecy; for she's here again, and I must love her, in spite of me. And since I must, I have this comfort, that the greatest wits are commonly the greatest cullies; because neither of the sexes can be wiser than some certain parts about them will give them leave.

PHAEDRA - Well, Sosia, and how go matters?

MERCURY - Our army is victorious.

PHAEDRA - And my servant, judge Gripus?

MERCURY - A voluptuous gormand.

PHAEDRA - But has he gotten wherewithal to be voluptuous; is he wealthy?

MERCURY - He sells justice as he uses; fleeces the rich rebels, and hangs up the poor.

PHAEDRA - Then, while he has money, he may make love to me. Has he sent me no token?

MERCURY - Yes, a kiss; and by the same token I am to give it you, as a remembrance from him.

PHAEDRA - How now, impudence! A beggarly serving-man presume to kiss me?

MERCURY - Suppose I were a god, and should make love to you?

PHAEDRA - I would first be satisfied, whether you were a poor god, or a rich god.

MERCURY - Suppose I were Mercury, the god of merchandise?

PHAEDRA - What! the god of small wares, and fripperies, of pedlers and pilferers?

MERCURY - How the gipsy despises me! [Aside.

PHAEDRA - I had rather you were Plutus, the god of money; or Jupiter, in a golden shower: there was a god for us women! he had the art of making love. Dost thou think that kings, or gods either, get mistresses by their good faces? no, it is the gold, and the presents they can make; there is the prerogative they have over their fair subjects.

MERCURY - All this notwithstanding, I must tell you, pretty Phædra, I am desperately in love with you.

PHAEDRA - And I must tell thee, ugly Sosia, thou hast not wherewithal to be in love.

MERCURY - Yes, a poor man may be in love, I hope.

PHAEDRA - I grant a poor rogue may be in love, but he can never make love. Alas, Sosia, thou hast neither face to invite me, nor youth to please me, nor gold to bribe me; and, besides all this, thou hast a wife, poor miserable Sosia!—What, ho, Bromia!

MERCURY - O thou merciless creature, why dost thou conjure up that sprite of a wife?

PHAEDRA - To rid myself of that devil of a poor lover. Since you are so lovingly disposed, I'll put you together to exercise your fury upon your own wedlock.—What, Bromia, I say, make haste; here is a vessel of yours, full freighted, that is going off without paying duties.

MERCURY - Since thou wilt not let me steal custom, she shall have all the cargo I have gotten in the wars; but thou mightst have lent me a little creek, to smuggle in.

PHAEDRA - Why, what have you gotten, good gentleman soldier, besides a legion of— [Snaps her fingers.

MERCURY - When the enemy was routed, I had the plundering of a tent.

PHAEDRA - That is to say, a house of canvas, with moveables of straw.—Make haste, Bromia!——

MERCURY - But it was the general's own tent.

PHAEDRA - You durst not fight, I am certain; and therefore came last in, when the rich plunder was gone beforehand.—Will you come, Bromia?

MERCURY - Pr'ythee, do not call so loud:—A great goblet, that holds a gallon.

PHAEDRA - Of what was that goblet made? answer quickly, for I am just calling very loud—Bro—

MERCURY - Of beaten gold. Now, call aloud, if thou dost not like the metal.

PHAEDRA - Bromia. [Very softly.

MERCURY - That struts in this fashion, with his arms a-kimbo, like a city magistrate; and a great bouncing belly, like a hostess with child of a kilderkin of wine. Now, what say you to that present, Phædra?

PHAEDRA - Why, I am considering—

MERCURY - What, I pr'ythee?

PHAEDRA - Why, how to divide the business equally; to take the gift, and refuse the giver, thou art so damnably ugly, and so old.

MERCURY - Now the devil take Jupiter, for confining me to this ungodly shape to-day! [Aside.] but Gripus is as old and as ugly too.

PHAEDRA - But Gripus is a person of quality, and my lady's uncle; and if he marries me, I shall take place of my lady. Hark, your wife! she has sent her tongue before her. I hear the thunderclap already; there is a storm approaching.

MERCURY - Yes, of thy brewing; I thank thee for it. O how I should hate thee now, if I could leave loving thee!

PHAEDRA - Not a word of the dear golden goblet, as you hope for—you know what, Sosia.

MERCURY - You give me hope, then—

PHAEDRA - Not absolutely hope neither; but gold is a great cordial in love matters; and the more you apply of it, the better.—[Aside.] I am honest, that is certain; but when I weigh my honesty against the goblet, I am not quite resolved on which side the scale will turn. [Exit PHAEDRA.

MERCURY - [Aloud.] Farewell, Phædra; remember me to my wife, and tell her—

Enter BROMIA.

BROMIA - Tell her what, traitor? that you are going away without seeing her?

MERCURY - That I am doing my duty, and following my master.

BROMIA - 'Umph!—so brisk, too! your master did his duty to my lady before he parted: He could leave his army in the lurch, and come galloping home at midnight to have a lick at the honey-pot; and steal to-bed as quietly as any mouse, I warrant you. My master knew what belonged to a married life; but you, sirrah, you trencher-carrying rascal, you worse than dunghill-cock; that stood clapping your wings, and crowing without doors, when you should have been at roost, you villain—

MERCURY - Hold your peace, dame Partlet, and leave your cackling; my master charged me to stand centry without doors.

BROMIA - My master! I dare swear thou beliest him; my master is more a gentleman than to lay such an unreasonable command upon a poor distressed married couple, and after such an absence too. No, there is no comparison between my master and thee, thou sneaksby.

MERCURY - No more than there is betwixt my lady and you, Bromia. You and I have had our time in a civil way, spouse, and much good love has been betwixt us; but we have been married fifteen years, I take it; and that hoighty toighty business ought, in conscience, to be over.

BROMIA - Marry come up, my saucy companion! I am neither old nor ugly enough to have that said to me.

MERCURY - But will you hear reason, Bromia? my lord and my lady are yet in a manner bride and bridegroom; they are in honey-moon still: do but think, in decency, what a jest it would be to the family, to see two venerable old married people lying snug in a bed together, and sighing out fine tender things to one another!

BROMIA - How now, traitor, darest thou maintain that I am past the age of having fine things said to me?

MERCURY - Not so, my dear; but certainly I am past the age of saying them.

BROMIA - Thou deservest not to be yoked with a woman of honour, as I am, thou perjured villain.

MERCURY - Ay, you are too much a woman of honour, to my sorrow; many a poor husband would be glad to compound for less honour in his wife, and more quiet. Pr'ythee, be but honest and continent in thy tongue, and do thy worst with every thing else about thee.

BROMIA - Thou wouldst have a woman of the town, wouldst thou! to be always speaking my husband fair, to make him digest his cuckoldom more easily! wouldst thou be a wittol, with a vengeance to thee? I am resolved I'll scour thy hide for that word. [Holds up her ladle at him.

MERCURY - Thou wilt not strike thy lord and husband, wilt thou?

BROMIA - Since thou wilt none of the meat, 'tis but justice to give thee the bastings of the ladle. [She courses him about.

MERCURY - [Running about.] Was ever poor deity so hen-pecked as I am! nay, then 'tis time to charm her asleep with my enchanted rod, before I am disgraced or ravished. [Plucks out his Caduceus, and strikes her upon the shoulder with it.

BROMIA - What, art thou rebelling against thy anointed wife! I'll make thee—how now—What, has the rogue bewitched me! I grow dull and stupid on the sudden—I can neither stir hand nor foot—I am just like him—I have lost the use of all my—members—[Yawning.]—I can't so much as wag my tongue—neither, and that's the last liv—ing part about a—woman— [Falls down.

MERCURY alone.

Lord, what have I suffered for being but a counterfeit married man one day! If ever I come to this house as a husband again—then—and yet that then was a lie too; for, while I am in love with this young gipsy, Phædra, I must return. But lie thou there, thou type of Juno; thou that wantest nothing of her tongue, but the immortality. If Jupiter ever let thee set foot in heaven, Juno will have a rattling second of thee; and there will never be a fair day in heaven or earth after it:

For two such tongues will break the poles asunder;
And, hourly scolding, make perpetual thunder.

[Exit MERCURY.

ACT III

SCENE I—Before Amphitryon's Palace

AMPHITRYON and SOSIA.

AMPHITRYON - Now, sirrah, follow me into the house; thou shalt be convinced at thy own cost, villain! What horrible lies hast thou told me! such improbabilities, such stuff, such nonsense!—that the monster, with two long horns, that frighted the great king, and the devil at the stone-cutter's, are truths to these.

SOSIA - I am but a slave, and you are master; and a poor man is always to lie when a rich man is pleased to contradict him: but, as sure as this is our house—

AMPHITRYON - So sure 'tis thy place of execution.—Thou art not made for lying neither.

SOSIA - That's certain; for all my neighbours say I have an honest face; or else they would never call me cuckold, as they do.

AMPHITRYON - I mean thou hast not wit enough to make a lie that will hang together: thou hast set up a trade that thou hast not stock enough to manage. O that I had but a crab-tree cudgel for thy sake!

SOSIA - How, a cudgel, said you! the devil take Jupiter for inventing that hard-hearted, merciless, knobby wood.

AMPHITRYON - The bitterness is yet to come: thou hast had but a half dose of it.

SOSIA - I was never good at swallowing physic; and my stomach wambles at the very thought of it. But, if I must have a second beating, in conscience let me strip first, that I may show you the black and blue streaks upon my sides and shoulders. I am sure I suffered them in your service.

AMPHITRYON - To what purpose wouldst thou show them?

SOSIA - Why, to the purpose that you may not strike me upon the sore places; and that, as he beat me the last night cross-ways, so you would please to beat me long-ways, to make clean work on't, that at least my skin may look like chequer-work.

AMPHITRYON - This request is too reasonable to be refused. But, that all things may be done in order, tell me over again the same story, with all the circumstances of thy commission, that a blow may follow in due form for every lie. To repetition, rogue; to repetition.

SOSIA - No; it shall be all a lie, if you please; and I'll eat my words, to save my shoulders.

AMPHITRYON - Ay, sirrah, now you find you are to be disproved; but 'tis too late. To repetition, rogue; to repetition.

SOSIA - With all my heart, to any repetition but the cudgel. But would you be pleased to answer me one civil question? Am I to use complaisance to you, as to a great person that will have all things said your own way? or am I to tell you the naked truth alone, without the ceremony of a farther beating?

AMPHITRYON - Nothing but the truth, and the whole truth; so help thee, cudgel!

SOSIA - That's a damned conclusion of a sentence: but, since it must be so—back and sides, at your own peril!—I set out from the port in an unlucky hour; the dusky canopy of night enveloping the hemisphere.

AMPHITRYON - [Strikes him.] Imprimis, for fustian:—now proceed.

SOSIA - I stand corrected: In plain prose then,—I went darkling, and whistling to keep myself from being afraid; mumbling curses betwixt my teeth, for being sent at such an unnatural time of night.

AMPHITRYON - How, sirrah, cursing and swearing against your lord and master! take— [Going to strike.

SOSIA - Hold, sir—pray, consider if this be not unreasonable to strike me for telling the whole truth, when you commanded me: I'll fall into my old dog-trot of lying again, if this must come of plain dealing.

AMPHITRYON - To avoid impertinences make an end of your journey, and come to the house;—what found you there, a god's name?

SOSIA - I came thither in no god's name at all, but in the devil's name; I found before the door a swinging fellow, with all my shapes and features, and accoutred also in my habit.

AMPHITRYON - Who was that fellow?

SOSIA - Who should it be, but another Sosia! a certain kind of other me: who knew all my unfortunate commission, precisely to a word, as well as I Sosia; as being sent by yourself from the port upon the same errand to Alcmena.

AMPHITRYON - What gross absurdities are these?

SOSIA - O Lord, O Lord, what absurdities!—as plain as any packstaff. That other me had posted himself there before me, me.—You won't give a man leave to speak poetically now; or else I would say, that I was arrived at the door just before I came thither.

AMPHITRYON - This must either be a dream or drunkenness, or madness in thee. Leave your buffooning and lying; I am not in humour to bear it, sirrah.

SOSIA - I would you should know I scorn a lie, and am a man of honour in every thing but just fighting. I tell you once again, in plain sincerity and simplicity of heart, that, before last night, I never took myself but for one single individual Sosia; but, coming to our door, I found myself, I know not how, divided, and, as it were, split into two Sosias.

AMPHITRYON - Leave buffooning: I see you would make me laugh, but you play the fool scurvily.

SOSIA - That may be; but, if I am a fool, I am not the only fool in this company.

AMPHITRYON - How now, impudence! I shall—

SOSIA - Be not in wrath, sir; I meant not you: I cannot possibly be the only fool; for, if I am one fool, I must certainly be two fools; because, as I told you, I am double.

AMPHITRYON - That one should be two, is very probable!

SOSIA - Have you not seen a six-pence split into two halves, by some ingenious school-boy, which bore on either side the impression of the monarch's face? Now, as those moieties were two three-pences, and yet in effect but one six-pence—

AMPHITRYON - No more of your villainous tropes and figures.

SOSIA - Nay, if an orator must be disarmed of his similitudes—

AMPHITRYON - A man had need of patience, to endure this gibberish! be brief, and come to a conclusion.

SOSIA - What would you have, sir? I came thither, but the t'other I was before me; for that there was two I's, is as certain, as that I have two eyes in this head of mine. This I, that am here, was weary: the t'other I was fresh; this I was peaceable, and t'other I was a hectoring bully I.

AMPHITRYON - And thou expect'st I should believe thee?

SOSIA - No; I am not so unreasonable; for I could never have believed it myself, if I had not been well beaten into it: but a cudgel, you know, is a convincing argument in a brawny fist. What shall I say, but that I was compelled, at last, to acknowledge myself! I found that he was very I, without fraud, cozen, or deceit. Besides, I viewed myself, as in a mirror, from head to foot; he was handsome of a noble presence, a charming air, loose and free in all his motions; and saw he was so much I, that I should have reason to be better satisfied with my own person, if his hands had not been a little of the heaviest.

AMPHITRYON - Once again, to a conclusion: Say you passed by him, and entered into the house.

SOSIA - I am a friend to truth, and say no such thing; he defended the door, and I could not enter.

AMPHITRYON - How, not enter?

SOSIA - Why, how should I enter? unless I were a spirit, to glide by him, and shoot myself through locks, and bolts, and two-inch boards.

AMPHITRYON - O coward! Didst thou not attempt to pass?

SOSIA - Yes, and was repulsed and beaten for my pains.

AMPHITRYON - Who beat thee?

SOSIA - I beat me.

AMPHITRYON - Didst thou beat thyself?

SOSIA - I don't mean I, here: but the absent Me beat me here present.

AMPHITRYON - There's no end of this intricate piece of nonsense.

SOSIA - 'Tis only nonsense, because I speak it, who am a poor fellow; but it would be sense, and substantial sense, if a great man said it, that was backed with a title, and the eloquence of ten thousand pounds a-year.

AMPHITRYON - No more; but let us enter:—Hold! my Alcmena is coming out, and has prevented me: how strangely will she be surprised to see me here so unexpectedly!

Enter ALCMENA and PHAEDRA.

ALCMENA - [To PHAEDRA.] Make haste after me to the temple; that we may thank the gods for this glorious success, which Amphitryon has had against the rebels—O heaven! [Seeing him.

AMPHITRYON - Those heavens, and all the blessed inhabitants, [Saluting her.
Grant, that the sweet rewarder of my pains
May still be kind, as on our nuptial night!

ALCMENA - So soon returned!

AMPHITRYON - So soon returned! Is this thy welcome home? [Stepping back.
So soon returned, says I am come unwished.
This is no language of desiring love:
Love reckons hours for months, and days for years;
And every little absence is an age.

ALCMENA - What says my lord?

AMPHITRYON - No, my Alcmena, no:
True love by its impatience measures time,
And the dear object never comes too soon.

ALCMENA - Nor ever came you so, nor ever shall;
But you yourself are changed from what you were,
Palled in desires, and surfeited of bliss.
Not so I met you at your last return;
When yesternight I flew into your arms,
And melted in your warm embrace.

AMPHITRYON - How's this?

ALCMENA - Did not my soul even sparkle at my eyes,

And shoot itself into your much-loved bosom?
Did I not tremble with excess of joy?
Nay agonize with pleasure at your sight,
With such inimitable proofs of passion,
As no false love could feign?

AMPHITRYON - What's this you tell me?

ALCMENA - Far short of truth, by heaven!
And you returned those proofs with usury;
And left me, with a sigh, at break of day.
Have you forgot?

AMPHITRYON - Or have you dreamt, Alcmena?
Perhaps some kind, revealing deity
Has whispered, in your sleep, the pleasing news
Of my return, and you believed it real;
Perhaps too, in your dream, you used me kindly;
And my preventing image reaped the joys
You meant, awake, to me.

ALCMENA - Some melancholy vapour, sure, has seized
Your brain, Amphitryon, and disturbed your sense;
Or yesternight is not so long a time,
But yet you might remember; and not force
An honest blush into my glowing cheeks,
For that which lawful marriage makes no crime.

AMPHITRYON - I thank you for my melancholy vapour.

ALCMENA - 'Tis but a just requital for my dream.

PHAEDRA - I find my master took too much of the creature last night, [Aside.] and now is angling for a quarrel, that no more may be expected from him to-night, when he has no assets.

[In the mean time, AMPHITRYON and ALCMENA - walk by themselves, and frown at each other as they meet.

AMPHITRYON - You dare not justify it to my face.

ALCMENA - Not what?

AMPHITRYON - That I returned before this hour.

ALCMENA - You dare not, sure, deny you came last night, And staid till break of day?

AMPHITRYON - O impudence!—Why Sosia!

SOSIA - Nay, I say nothing; for all things here may go by enchantment, as they did with me, for aught I know.

ALCMENA - Speak, Phædra,—was he here?

PHAEDRA - You know, madam, I am but a chamber-maid; and, by my place, I am to forget all that was done over night in love-matters,—unless my master please to rub up my memory with another diamond.

AMPHITRYON - Now, in the name of all the gods, Alcmena,
A little recollect your scattered thoughts,
And weigh what you have said.

ALCMENA - I weighed it well, Amphitryon, ere I spoke:
And she, and Bromia, all the slaves and servants,
Can witness they beheld you, when you came.
If other proof were wanting, tell me how
I came to know your fight, your victory,
The death of Pterelas in single combat?
And farther, from whose hands I had a jewel,
The spoils of him you slew?

AMPHITRYON - This is amazing!
Have I already given you those diamonds,
The present I reserved?

ALCMENA - 'Tis an odd question:
You see I wear them; look.

AMPHITRYON - Now answer, Sosia.

SOSIA - Yes, now I can answer with a safe conscience, as to that point; all the rest may be art magic, but, as for the diamonds, here they are, under safe custody.

ALCMENA - Then what are these upon my arm? [To SOSIA.

SOSIA - Flints, or pebbles, or some such trumpery of enchanted stones.

PHAEDRA - They say, the proof of a true diamond is to glitter in the dark: I think my master had best take my lady into some by-corner, and try whose diamond will sparkle best.

SOSIA - Yet, now I think on't, madam, did not a certain friend of mine present them to you?

ALCMENA - What friend?

SOSIA - Why another Sosia, one that made himself Sosia in my despite, and also unsosiated me.

AMPHITRYON - Sirrah, leave your nauseous nonsense; break open the seal, and take out the diamonds.

SOSIA - More words than one to a bargain, sir. I I thank you,—that's no part of prudence for me to commit burglary upon the seals: Do you look first upon the signet, and tell me, in your conscience, whether the seals be not as firm as when you clapt the wax upon them.

AMPHITRYON - The signature is firm. [Looking.

SOSIA - Then take the signature into your own custody, and open it; for I will have nothing done at my proper peril. [Giving him the Casket.

AMPHITRYON - O heavens! here's nothing but an empty space, the nest where they were laid. [Breaking open the Seal.

SOSIA - Then, if the birds are flown, the fault's not mine. Here has been fine conjuring work; or else the jewel, knowing to whom it should be given, took occasion to steal out, by a natural instinct, and tied itself to that pretty arm.

AMPHITRYON - Can this be possible?

SOSIA - Yes, very possible: You, my lord Amphitryon, may have brought forth another. You my lord Amphitryon, as well as I, Sosia, have brought forth another Me, Sosia; and our diamonds may have procreated these diamonds, and so we are all three double.

PHAEDRA - If this be true, I hope my goblet has gigged another golden goblet; and then they may carry double upon all four. [Aside.

ALCMENA - My lord, I have stood silent, out of wonder
What you could wonder at.

AMPHITRYON - A chilling sweat, a damp of jealousy,
Hangs on my brows, and clams upon my limbs.
I fear, and yet I must be satisfied;
And, to be satisfied, I must dissemble. [Aside.

ALCMENA - Why muse you so, and murmur to yourself?
If you repent your bounty, take it back.

AMPHITRYON - Not so; but, if you please, relate what past
At our last interview.

ALCMENA - That question would infer you were not here.

AMPHITRYON - I say not so;
I only would refresh my memory,
And have my reasons to desire the story.

PHAEDRA - So, this is as good sport for me, as an examination of a great belly before a magistrate.

ALCMENA - The story is not long: you know I met you,
Kissed you, and pressed you close within my arms,
With all the tenderness of wifely love.

AMPHITRYON - I could have spared that kindness.— [Aside.
And what did I?

ALCMENA - You strained me with a masculine embrace,

As you would squeeze my soul out.

AMPHITRYON - Did I so?

ALCMENA - You did.

AMPHITRYON - Confound those arms that were so kind!— [Aside. Proceed, proceed— [To her.

ALCMENA - You would not stay to sup; but much complaining of your drowsiness, and want of natural rest—

AMPHITRYON - Made haste to bed: Ha, was't not so?
Go on—
[Aside.] And stab me with each syllable thou speak'st.

PHAEDRA - So, now 'tis coming, now 'tis coming.

ALCMENA - I have no more to say.

AMPHITRYON - Why, went we not to bed?

ALCMENA - Why not?
Is it a crime for husband and for wife
To go to bed, my lord?

AMPHITRYON - Perfidious woman!

ALCMENA - Ungrateful man!

AMPHITRYON - She justifies it too!

ALCMENA - I need not justify: Of what am I accused?

AMPHITRYON - Of all that prodigality of kindness
Given to another, and usurped from me.
So bless me, Heaven, if, since my first departure,
I ever set my foot upon this threshold!
So am I innocent of all those joys,
And dry of those embraces.

ALCMENA - Then I, it seems, am false!

AMPHITRYON - As surely false, as what thou say'st is true.

ALCMENA - I have betrayed my honour, and my love,
And am a foul adultress?

AMPHITRYON - What thou art,
Thou stand'st condemned to be, by thy relation.

ALCMENA - Go, thou unworthy man! for ever go:

No more my husband: go, thou base impostor!
Who tak'st a vile pretence to taint my fame,
And, not content to leave, wouldst ruin me.
Enjoy thy wished divorce: I will not plead
My innocence of this pretended crime;
I need not. Spit thy venom; do thy worst;
But know, the more thou wouldst expose my virtue,
Like purest linen laid in open air,
'Twill bleach the more, and whiten to the view.

AMPHITRYON - 'Tis well thou art prepared for thy divorce:
For, know thou too, that, after this affront,
This foul indignity done to my honour,
Divorcement is but petty reparation.
But, since thou hast, with impudence, affirmed
My false return, and bribed my slaves to vouch it,
The truth shall, in the face of Thebes, be cleared:
Thy uncle, the companion of my voyage,
And all the crew of seamen shall be brought,
Who were embarked, and came with me to land,
Nor parted, till I reached this cursed door:
So shall this vision of my late return
Stand a detected lie; and woe to those,
Who thus betrayed my honour!

SOSIA - Sir, shall I wait on you?

AMPHITRYON - No, I will go alone. Expect me here. [Exit AMPHITRYON.

PHAEDRA - Please you, that I— [To Alcmena.

ALCMENA - Oh! nothing now can please me:
Darkness, and solitude, and sighs, and tears,
And all the inseparable train of grief,
Attend my steps for ever. [Exit ALCMENA.

SOSIA - What if I should lie now, and say we have been here before? I never saw any good that came of telling truth. [Aside.

PHAEDRA - He makes no more advances to me: I begin a little to suspect, that my gold goblet will prove but copper. [Aside.

SOSIA - Yes, 'tis resolved, I will lie abominably, against the light of my own conscience. For, suppose the other Sosia has been here, perhaps that strong dog has not only beaten me, but also has been predominant upon my wife, and most carnally misused her! Now, by asking certain questions of her, with a side-wind, I may come to understand how squares go, and whether my nuptial bed be violated. [Aside.

PHAEDRA - Most certainly he has learned impudence of his master, and will deny his being here; but that shall not serve his turn, to cheat me of my present. [Aside.]—Why, Sosia! What, in a brown study?

SOSIA - A little cogitabund, or so, concerning this dismal revolution in our family.

PHAEDRA - But that should not make you neglect your duty to me, your mistress.

SOSIA - Pretty soul! I would thou wert, upon condition that old Bromia were six foot under ground.

PHAEDRA - What! is all your hot courtship to me dwindled into a poor unprofitable wish? You may remember, I did not bid you absolutely despair.

SOSIA - No, for all things yet may be accommodated, in an amicable manner, betwixt my master and my lady.

PHAEDRA - I mean, to the business betwixt you and me—

SOSIA - Why, I hope we two never quarrelled?

PHAEDRA - Must I remember you of a certain promise, that you made me at our last parting?

SOSIA - Oh, when I went to the army: that I should still be praising thy beauty to judge Gripus, and keep up his affections to thee?

PHAEDRA - No, I mean the business betwixt you and me this morning—that you promised me—

SOSIA - That I promised thee—I find it now. That strong dog, my brother Sosia, has been here before me, and made love to her. [Aside.

PHAEDRA - You are considering, whether or no you should keep your promise—

SOSIA - That I should keep my promise. The truth on't is, she's another-guess morsel than old Bromia. [Aside.

PHAEDRA - And I had rather you should break it, in a manner, and as it were, and in some sense—

SOSIA - In a manner, and as it were, and in some sense, thou say'st?—I find, the strong dog has only tickled up her imagination, and not enjoyed her; so that, with my own limbs, I may perform the sweetness of his function with her. [Aside.]—No, sweet creature, the promise shall not be broken; but what I have undertaken, I will perform like a man of honour.

PHAEDRA - Then you remember the preliminaries of the present—

SOSIA - Yes, yes, in gross I do remember something; but this disturbance of the family has somewhat stupified my memory. Some pretty quelque chose, I warrant thee; some acceptable toy, of small value.

PHAEDRA - You may call a gold goblet a toy; but I put a greater value upon your presents.

SOSIA - A gold goblet, say'st thou! Yes, now I think on't, it was a kind of a gold goblet, as a gratuity after consummation.

PHAEDRA - No, no; I had rather make sure of one bribe beforehand, than be promised ten gratuities.

SOSIA - Yes, now I remember, it was, in some sense, a gold goblet, by way of earnest; and it contained—

PHAEDRA - One large—

SOSIA - How, one large—

PHAEDRA - Gallon.

SOSIA - No; that was somewhat too large, in conscience: It was not a whole gallon; but it may contain, reasonably speaking, one large—thimble-full; but gallons and thimble-fulls are so like, that, in speaking, I might easily mistake them.

PHAEDRA - Is it come to this?—Out, traitor!

SOSIA - I had been a traitor, indeed, to have betrayed thee to the swallowing of a gallon; but a thimble-full of cordial water is easily sipt off: and then, this same goblet is so very light too, that it will be no burden to carry it about with thee in thy pocket.

PHAEDRA - O apostate to thy love! O perjured villain!—

Enter Bromia.

What, are you here, Bromia? I was telling him his own: I was giving him a rattle for his treacheries to you, his love: You see I can be a friend, upon occasion.

BROMIA - Ay, chicken, I never doubted of thy kindness; but, for this fugitive—this rebel—this miscreant—

SOSIA - A kind welcome, to an absent lover, as I have been.

BROMIA - Ay; and a kind greeting you gave me, at your return; when you used me so barbarously this morning.

SOSIA - The t'other Sosia has been with her too; and has used her barbarously: barbarously,—that is to say, uncivilly: and uncivilly,—I am afraid that means too civilly. [Aside.

PHAEDRA - You had best deny you were here this morning! And by the same token—

SOSIA - Nay, no more tokens, for Heaven's sake, dear Phædra. Now must I ponder with myself a little, whether it be better for me to have been here, or not to have been here, this morning. [Aside.

Enter a Servant.

SERVANT - Phædra, my lord's without; and will not enter till he has first spoken with you. [Exit Serv.

PHAEDRA - [To him in private.] Oh, that I could stay to help worry thee for this abuse; but the best on't is, I leave thee in good hands.—Farewell, Thimble—To him, Bromia. [Exit Phædra.

BROMIA - No; you did not beat me, and put me into a swoon, and deprive me of the natural use of my tongue for a long half hour: you did not beat me down with your little wand:—but I shall teach you to use your rod another time—I shall.

SOSIA - Put her into a swoon, with my little wand, and so forth! That's more than ever I could do. These are terrible circumstances, that some Sosia or other has been here. Now, if he has literally beaten her, gramercy, brother Sosia! he has but done what I would have done, if I had durst. But I am afraid it was only a damned love-figure; and that the wand, that laid her asleep, might signify the peace-maker. [Aside.

BROMIA - Now you are snuffling up on a cold scent, for some pitiful excuse. I know you; twenty to one, but you will plead a drunkenness; you are used to be pot-valiant.

SOSIA - I was pumping, and I thank her, she has invented for me.—Yes, Bromia, I must confess I was exalted; and, possibly, I might scour upon thee, or perhaps be a little more familiar with thy person, by the way of kindness, than if I had been sober: but, pr'ythee, inform me what I did, that I may consider what satisfaction I am to make thee.

BROMIA - Are you there at your dog-tricks! You would be forgetting, would you? like a drunken bully that affronts over night, and, when he is called to account the next morning, remembers nothing of the quarrel; and asks pardon, to avoid fighting.

SOSIA - By Bacchus, I was overtaken; but I should be loth that I committed any folly with thee.

BROMIA - I am sure, I kept myself awake all night, that I did, in expectation of your coming. [Crying.

SOSIA - But what amends did I make thee, when I came?

BROMIA - You know well enough, to my sorrow, but that you play the hypocrite.

SOSIA - I warrant, I was monstrous kind to thee.

BROMIA - Yes, monstrous kind indeed: You never said a truer word; for, when I came to kiss you, you pulled away your mouth, and turned your cheek to me.

SOSIA - Good.

BROMIA - How, good! Here's fine impudence! He justifies!

SOSIA - Yes, I do justify, that I turned my cheek, like a prudent person, that my breath might not offend thee; for, now I remember, I had eaten garlick.

BROMIA - Ay, you remember, and forget, just as it makes for you, or against you; but, to mend the matter, you never spoke one civil word to me; but stood like a stock, without sense or motion.

SOSIA - Yet better. [Aside.

BROMIA - After which, I lovingly invited you to take your place in your nuptial bed, as the laws of matrimony oblige you; and you inhumanly refused me.

SOSIA - Ay, there's the main point of the business! Art thou morally certain, that I refused thee? Look me now in the face, and say I did not commit matrimony with thee!

BROMIA - I wonder how thou canst look me in the face, after that refusal!

SOSIA - Say it once again, that I did not feloniously come to bed to thee!

BROMIA - No, thou cold traitor, thou know'st thou didst not.

SOSIA - Best of all!—'twas discreetly done of me to abstain.

BROMIA - What, do you insult upon me too?

SOSIA - No, I do not insult upon you—but—

BROMIA - But what? How was it discreetly done then? ha!

SOSIA - Because it is the received opinion of physicians, that nothing but puling chits, and booby-fools are procreated in drunkenness.

BROMIA - A received opinion, snivel-guts! I'll be judged by all the married women of this town, if any one of them has received it. The devil take the physicians for meddling in our matters! If a husband will be ruled by them, there are five weeks of abstinence in dog-days too; for fear a child, that was got in August, should be born just nine months after, and be blear-eyed, like a May kitten.

SOSIA - Let the physicians alone; they are honest men, whatever the world says of them. But, for a certain reason, that I best know, I am glad that matter ended so fairly and peaceably betwixt us.

BROMIA - Yes, 'twas very fair and peaceably; to strike a woman down, and beat her most outrageously.

SOSIA - Is't possible that I drubbed thee?

BROMIA - I find your drift; you would fain be provoking me to a new trial now: but, i'faith, you shall bring me to no more handy-blows; I shall make bold to trust to my tongue hereafter. You never durst have offered to hold up a finger against me, till you went a trooping.

SOSIA - Then I am a conqueror; and I laud my own courage: this renown I have achieved by soldier-ship and stratagem. Know your duty, spouse, hence-forward, to your supreme commander. [Strutting.

Enter JUPITER and PHAEDRA, attended by Musicians and Dancers.

PHAEDRA - Indeed I wondered at your quick return.

JUPITER - Even so almighty love will have it, Phædra;
And the stern goddess of sweet-bitter cares,
Who bows our necks beneath her brazen yoke.
I would have manned my heart, and held it out;
But, when I thought of what I had possessed,
Those joys, that never end, but to begin,

O, I am all on fire to make my peace;
And die, Jove knows, as much as I can die,
Till I am reconciled.

PHAEDRA - I fear 'twill be in vain.

JUPITER - 'Tis difficult:
But nothing is impossible to love;
To love like mine; for I have proved his force,
And my Alcmena too has felt his dart.
If I submit, there's hope.

PHAEDRA - 'Tis possible I may solicit for you.

JUPITER - But wilt thou promise me to do thy best?

PHAEDRA - Nay, I promise nothing—unless you begin to promise first. [Curtsying.

JUPITER - I will not be ungrateful.

PHAEDRA - Well; I'll try to bring her to the window; you shall have a fair shot at her; if you can bring her down, you are a good marksman.

JUPITER - That's all I ask;
And I will so reward thee, gentle Phædra—

PHAEDRA - What, with catsguts and rosin! This Solla is but a lamentable empty sound.

JUPITER - Then, there's a sound will please thee better. [Throwing her a purse.

PHAEDRA - Ay, there's something of melody in this sound. I could dance all day to the music of Chink, Chink.

JUPITER - Go, Sosia, round our Thebes,
To Polidas, to Tranio, and to Gripus,
Companions of our war; invite them all
To join their prayers to smooth Alcmena's brow,
And, with a solemn feast, to crown the day.

SOSIA - [Taking Jupiter about the knees.] Let me embrace you, sir. [Jupiter pushes him away.] Nay, you must give me leave to express my gratitude; I have not eaten, to say eating, nor drunk, to say drinking, never since our villainous encamping so near the enemy. It is true, I escaped the bloody-flux, because I had so little in my bowels to come out; and I durst let nothing go, in conscience, because I had nothing to swallow in the room on't.

JUPITER - You, Bromia, see that all things be prepared, With that magnificence, as if some god Were guest or master here.

SOSIA - Or rather, as much as if twenty gods were to be guests or masters here.

BROMIA - That you may eat for to-day and to-morrow.

SOSIA - Or, rather again, for to-day and yesterday, and as many months backward, as I am indebted to my own belly.

JUPITER - Away, both of you.

[Exeunt SOSIA and BROMIA severally.

Now I have packed him hence, thou other Sosia,
(Who, though thou art not present, hear'st my voice)
Be ready to attend me at my call,
And to supply his place.

Enter MERCURY to JUPITER; ALCMENA and PHAEDRA appear above.

See, she appears: [Seeing ALCMENA.
This is my bribe to Phædra; when I made
This gold, I made a greater God than Jove,
And gave my own omnipotence away.

JUPITER signs to the Musicians. Song and Dance: After which, Alcmena withdraws, frowning.

SONG.
I.
Celia, that I once was blest
Is now the torment of my breast;
Since, to curse me, you bereave me
Of the pleasures I possest:
Cruel creature, to deceive me!
First to love, and then to leave me!

II.
Had you the bliss refused to grant,
Then I had never known the want:
But possessing once the blessing,
Is the cause of my complaint;
Once possessing is but tasting;
'Tis no bliss that is not lasting.

III.
Celia now is mine no more;
But I am her's, and must adore,
Nor to leave her will endeavour;
Charms, that captived me before,
No unkindness can dissever;
Love, that's true, is love for ever.

JUPITER - O stay.

MERCURY - She's gone; and seemed to frown at parting.

JUPITER - Follow, and thou shalt see her soon appeased;
For I, who made her, know her inward state;
No woman, once well-pleased, can throughly hate.
I gave them beauty to subdue the strong,—
A mighty empire, but it lasts not long.
I gave them pride, to make mankind their slave;
But, in exchange, to men I flattery gave.
The offending lover, when he lowest lies,
Submits, to conquer; and but kneels, to rise.

ACT IV

SCENE I

JUPITER following ALCMENA; MERCURY and PHAEDRA.

JUPITER - O stay, my dear Alcmena; hear me speak!

ALCMENA - No, I would fly thee to the ridge of earth,
And leap the precipice, to 'scape thy sight.

JUPITER - For pity—

ALCMENA - Leave me, thou ungrateful man.

JUPITER - I cannot leave you; no, but like a ghost,
Whom your unkindness murdered, will I haunt you.

ALCMENA - Once more, be gone; I'm odious to myself,
For having loved thee once.

JUPITER - Hate not, the best and fairest of your kind!
Nor can you hate your lover, though you would:
Your tears, that fall so gently, are but grief:
There may be anger; but there must be love.
The dove, that murmurs at her mate's neglect,
But counterfeits a coyness, to be courted.

ALCMENA - Courtship from thee, and after such affronts!

JUPITER - Is this that everlasting love you vowed
Last night, when I was circled in your arms?
Remember what you swore.

ALCMENA - Think what thou wert, and who could swear too much?
Think what thou art, and that unswears it all.

JUPITER - Can you forsake me, for so small a fault?
'Twas but a jest, perhaps too far pursued;

'Twas but, at most, a trial of your faith,
How you could bear unkindness;
'Twas but to get a reconciling kiss,
A wanton stratagem of love.

ALCMENA - See how he doubles, like a hunted hare:
A jest, and then a trial, and a bait;
All stuff, and daubing!

JUPITER - Think me jealous, then.

ALCMENA - O that I could! for that's a noble crime,
And which a lover can with ease forgive;
'Tis the high pulse of passion in a fever;
A sickly draught, but shews a burning thirst:
Thine was a surfeit, not a jealousy;
And in that loathing of thy full-gorged love,
Thou saw'st the nauseous object with disdain.

JUPITER - O think not that! for you are ever new:
Your fruits of love are like eternal spring,
In happy climes, where some are in the bud,
Some green, and ripening some, while others fall.

ALCMENA - Ay, now you tell me this,
When roused desires, and fresh recruits of force,
Enable languished love to take the field:
But never hope to be received again;
You would again deny you were received,
And brand my spotless fame.

JUPITER - I will not dare to justify my crime,
But only point you where to lay the blame;
Impute it to the husband, not the lover.

ALCMENA - How vainly would the sophister divide,
And make the husband and the lover two!

JUPITER - Yes, 'tis the husband is the guilty wretch;
His insolence forgot the sweets of love,
And, deeming them his due, despised the feast.
Not so the famished lover could forget;
He knew he had been there, and had been blest
With all that hope could wish, or sense can bear.

ALCMENA - Husband and lover, both alike I hate.

JUPITER - And I confess I have deserved that hate.
Too charming fair, I kneel for your forgiveness: [Kneeling.
I beg, by those fair eyes
Which gave me wounds, that time can never cure,

Receive my sorrows, and restore my joys.

ALCMENA - Unkind, and cruel! I can speak no more.

JUPITER - O give it vent, Alcmena, give it vent;
I merit your reproach, I would be cursed;
Let your tongue curse me, while your heart forgives.

ALCMENA - Can I forget such usage?

JUPITER - Can you hate me?

ALCMENA - I'll do my best; for sure I ought to hate you.

JUPITER - That word was only hatched upon your tongue,
It came not from your heart. But try again,
And if, once more, you can but say,—I hate you,
My sword shall do you justice.

ALCMENA - Then—I hate you.

JUPITER - Then you pronounce the sentence of my death.

ALCMENA - I hate you much, but yet—I love you more.

JUPITER - To prove that love, then say, that you forgive me;
For there remains but this alternative,
Resolve to pardon, or to punish me.

ALCMENA - Alas! what I resolve appears too plain;
In saying that I cannot hate, I pardon.

JUPITER - But what's a pardon worth without a seal?
Permit me, in this transport of my joy—[Kisses her hand.

ALCMENA - Forbear; I am offended with myself,
[Putting him gently away with her hand.
That I have shewn this weakness.—Let me go,
Where I may blush alone;— [Going, and looking back on him.
But come not you,
Lest I should spoil you with excess of fondness,
And let you love again. [Exit ALCMENA.

JUPITER - Forbidding me to follow, she invites me:—
This is the mould of which I made the sex:
I gave them but one tongue, to say us nay;
And two kind eyes to grant.—Be sure that none
Approach, to interrupt our privacy. [To MERCURY.

[Exit JUPITER after ALCMENA.

MERCURY and PHAEDRA remain.

MERCURY - Your lady has made the challenge of reconciliation to my lord: here's a fair example for us two, Phædra.

PHAEDRA - No example at all, Sosia; for my lady had the diamonds beforehand, and I have none of the gold goblet.

MERCURY - The goblet shall be forthcoming, if thou wilt give me weight for weight.

PHAEDRA - Yes, and measure for measure too, Sosia; that is, for a thimble-full of gold, a thimble-full of love.

MERCURY - What think you now, Phædra? Here's a weighty argument of love for you.

[Pulling out the Goblet in a case from under his Cloak.

PHAEDRA - Now Jupiter, of his mercy, let me kiss thee, O thou dear metal!

[Taking it in both hands.

MERCURY - And Venus, of her mercy, let me kiss thee, dear, dear Phædra!

PHAEDRA - Not so fast, Sosia; there's a damned proverb in your way,—"Many things happen betwixt the cup and the lip," you know.

MERCURY - Why, thou wilt not cheat me of my goblet?

PHAEDRA - Yes, as sure as you would cheat me of my maidenhead: I am yet but just even with you, for the last trick you played me. And, besides, this is but a bare retaining fee; you must give me another before the cause is opened.

MERCURY - Shall I not come to your bed-side to-night?

PHAEDRA - No, nor to-morrow night neither; but this shall be my sweetheart in your place: 'tis a better bedfellow, and will keep me warmer in cold weather.

[Exit PHAEDRA.

MERCURY alone.

MERCURY - Now, what's the god of wit in a woman's hand? This very goblet I stole from Gripus; and he got it out of bribes, too. But this is the common fate of ill-gotten goods, that, as they came in by covetousness, they go out by whoring.—

Enter AMPHITRYON.

Oh, here's Amphitryon again; but I'll manage him above in the balcony [Exit MERCURY.

AMPHITRYON - Not one of those, I looked for, to be found,
As some enchantment hid them from my sight!

Perhaps, as Sosia says, 'tis witchcraft all.
Seals may be opened, diamonds may be stolen;
But how I came, in person, yesterday,
And gave that present to Alcmena's hands,
That which I never gave, nor ever came,—
O there's the rock on which my reason splits!
Would that were all! I fear my honour, too.
I'll try her once again;—she may be mad;—
A wretched remedy; but all I have,
To keep me from despair.

MERCURY - [From the Balcony, aside.] This is no very charitable action of a god, to use him ill, who has never offended me; but my planet disposes me to malice; and when we great persons do but a little mischief, the world has a good bargain of us.

AMPHITRYON - How now, what means the locking up of my doors at this time of day? [Knocks.

MERCURY - Softly, friend, softly; you knock as loud, and as saucily, as a lord's footman, that was sent before him to warn the family of his honour's visit. Sure you think the doors have no feeling! What the devil are you, that rap with such authority?

AMPHITRYON - Look out, and see; 'tis I.

MERCURY - You! what you?

AMPHITRYON - No more, I say, but open.

MERCURY - I'll know to whom first.

AMPHITRYON - I am one, that can command the doors open.

MERCURY - Then you had best command them, and try whether they will obey you.

AMPHITRYON - Dost thou not know me?

MERCURY - Pr'ythee, how should I know thee? Dost thou take me for a conjurer?

AMPHITRYON - What's this? midsummer-moon! Is all the world gone a madding?—Why, Sosia!

MERCURY - That's my name, indeed; didst thou think I had forgot it?

AMPHITRYON - Dost thou see me?

MERCURY - Why, dost thou pretend to go invisible? If thou hast any business here, dispatch it quickly; I have no leisure to throw away upon such prattling companions.

AMPHITRYON - Thy companion, slave! How darest thou use this insolent language to thy master?

MERCURY - How! Thou my master? By what title? I never had any other master but Amphitryon.

AMPHITRYON - Well; and for whom dost thou take me?

MERCURY - For some rogue or other; but what rogue I know not.

AMPHITRYON - Dost thou not know me for Amphitryon, slave!

MERCURY - How should I know thee, when I see thou dost not know thyself? Thou Amphitryon! In what tavern hast thou been? and how many bottles did thy business, to metamorphose thee into my lord?

AMPHITRYON - I will so drub thee for this insolence!

MERCURY - How now, impudence, are you threatening your betters? I should bring you to condign punishment, but that I have a great respect for the good wine, though I find it in a fool's noddle.

AMPHITRYON - What, none to let me in? Why, Phædra! Bromia!—

MERCURY - Peace, fellow; if my wife hears thee, we are both undone. At a word, Phædra and Bromia are very busy; one in making a caudle for my lady, and the other in heating napkins, to rub down my lord when he rises from bed.

AMPHITRYON - Amazement seizes me!

MERCURY - At what art thou amazed? My master and my lady had a falling out, and are retired, without seconds, to decide the quarrel. If thou wert not a meddlesome fool, thou wouldst not be thrusting thy nose into other people's matters. Get thee about thy business, if thou hast any; for I'll hear no more of thee.

[Exit MERCURY from above.

AMPHITRYON - Braved by my slave, dishonoured by my wife!
To what a desperate plunge am I reduced,
If this be true the villain says? But why
That feeble if! It must be true; she owns it.
Now, whether to conceal, or blaze the affront?
One way, I spread my infamy abroad;
And t'other, hide a burning coal within,
That preys upon my vitals: I can fix
On nothing, but on vengeance.

Enter SOSIA, POLIDAS, GRIPUS, and TRANIO.

GRIPUS - Yonder he is, walking hastily to and fro before his door, like a citizen clapping his sides before his shop in a frosty morning; 'tis to catch a stomach, I believe.

SOSIA - I begin to be afraid, that he has more stomach to my sides and shoulders, than to his own victuals. How he shakes his head, and stamps, and what strides he fetches! He's in one of his damned moods again; I don't like the looks of him.

AMPHITRYON - Oh, my mannerly, fair-spoken, obedient slave, are you there! I can reach you now without climbing: Now we shall try who's drunk, and who's sober.

SOSIA - Why this is as it should be: I was somewhat suspicious that you were in a pestilent humour. Yes, we will have a crash at the bottle, when your lordship pleases; I have summoned them, you see, and they are notable topers, especially judge Gripus.

GRIPUS - Yes, faith; I never refuse my glass in a good quarrel.

AMPHITRYON - [To SOSIA.] Why, thou insolent villain! I'll teach a slave how to use his master thus.

SOSIA - Here's a fine business towards! I am sure I ran as fast as ever my legs could carry me, to call them; nay, you may trust my diligence in all affairs belonging to the belly.

GRIPUS - He has been very faithful to his commission. I'll bear him witness.

AMPHITRYON - How can you be witness, where you were not present?—The balcony, sirrah! the balcony!

SOSIA - Why, to my best remembrance, you never invited the balcony.

AMPHITRYON - What nonsense dost thou plead, for an excuse of thy foul language, and thy base replies!

SOSIA - You fright a man out of his senses first, and blame him afterwards for talking nonsense! But it is better for me to talk nonsense, than for some to do nonsense; I will say that, whate'er comes on't. Pray, sir, let all things be done decently: what, I hope, when a man is to be hanged, he is not trussed upon the gallows, like a dumb dog, without telling him wherefore.

AMPHITRYON - By your pardon, gentlemen; I have no longer patience to forbear him.

SOSIA - Justice, justice!—My Lord Gripus, as you are a true magistrate, protect me. Here's a process of beating going forward, without sentence given.

GRIPUS - My Lord Amphitryon, this must not be; let me first understand the demerits of the criminal.

SOSIA - Hold you to that point, I beseech your honour, as you commiserate the case of a poor, innocent malefactor.

AMPHITRYON - To shut the door against me in my very face, to deny me entrance, to brave me from the balcony, to laugh at me, to threaten me! what proofs of innocence call you these? but if I punish not this insolence—

[Is going to beat him, and is held by POLIDAS and TRANIO.

I beg you, let me go.

SOSIA - I charge you, in the king's name, hold him fast; for you see he's bloodily disposed.

GRIPUS - Now, what hast thou to say for thyself, Sosia?

SOSIA - I say, in the first place, be sure you hold him, gentlemen; for I shall never plead worth one farthing, while I am bodily afraid.

POLIDAS - Speak boldly; I warrant thee.

SOSIA - Then if I may speak boldly, under my lord's favour, I do not say he lies neither: no, I am too well bred for that; but his lordship fibs most abominably.

AMPHITRYON - Do you hear his impudence? yet will you let me go?

SOSIA - No impudence at all, my lord; for how could I, naturally speaking, be in the balcony, and affronting you, when at the same time I was in every street of Thebes, inviting these gentlemen to dinner?

GRIPUS - Hold a little:—How long since was it that he spoke to you from the said balcony?

AMPHITRYON - Just now; not a minute before he brought you hither.

SOSIA - Now speak, my witnesses.

GRIPUS - I can answer for him for this last half hour.

POLIDAS - And I.

TRANIO - And I.

SOSIA - Now judge equitably, gentlemen, whether I was not a civil well-bred person, to tell my lord he fibs only?

AMPHITRYON - Who gave you that order, to invite them?

SOSIA - He that best might,—yourself: By the same token, you bid old Bromia provide an' 'twere for a god, and I put in for a brace, or a leash;—no, now I think on't, it was for ten couple of gods, to make sure of plenty.

AMPHITRYON - When did I give thee this pretended commission?

SOSIA - Why, you gave me this pretended commission, when you were just ready to give my lady the fiddles, and a dance; in order, as I suppose, to your second bedding.

AMPHITRYON - Where, in what place, did I give this order?

SOSIA - Here, in this place, in the presence of this very door, and of that balcony; and, if they could speak, they would both justify it.

AMPHITRYON - O, heaven! These accidents are so surprising, the more I think of them, the more I am lost in my imagination.

GRIPUS - Nay, he has told us some passages, as he came along, that seem to surpass the power of nature.

SOSIA - What think you now, my lord, of a certain twin-brother of mine, called Sosia? 'Tis a sly youth: pray heaven, you have not just such another relation within doors, called Amphitryon. It may be it was he that put upon me, in your likeness; and perhaps he may have put something upon your lordship too, that may weigh heavy upon the forehead.

AMPHITRYON - [To those who hold him.] Let me go; Sosia may be innocent, and I will not hurt him. Open the door, I'll resolve my doubts immediately.

SOSIA - The door is peremptory, that it will not be opened without keys; and my brother on the inside is in possession, and will not part with them.

AMPHITRYON - Then 'tis manifest that I am affronted.—Break open the door there.

GRIPUS - Stir not a man of you to his assistance.

AMPHITRYON - Dost thou take part with my adulteress too, because she is thy niece?

GRIPUS - I take part with nothing, but the law; and, to break the doors open, is to break the law.

AMPHITRYON - Do thou command them then.

GRIPUS - I command nothing without my warrant; and my clerk is not here to take his fees for drawing it.

AMPHITRYON - [Aside.] The devil take all justice-brokers! I curse him too, when I have been hunting him all over the town, to be my witness! But I'll bring soldiers, to force open the doors, by my own commission. [Exit Amph.

SOSIA - Pox o' these forms of law, to defeat a man of a dinner, when he's sharp set! 'Tis against the privilege of a free-born stomach; and is no less than subversion of fundamentals. [Jupiter above in the Balcony.

JUPITER - Oh, my friends, I am sorry I have made you wait so long: you are welcome; and the door shall be opened to you immediately. [Exit Jupiter.

GRIPUS - Was not that Amphitryon?

SOSIA - Why, who should it be else?

GRIPUS - In all appearance it was he; but how got be thither?

POLIDAS - In such a trice too!

TRANIO - And after he had just left us!

GRIPUS - And so much altered, for the better, in his humour!

SOSIA - Here's such a company of foolish questions, when a man's hungry! You had best stay dinner, till he has proved himself to be Amphitryon in form of law: but I'll make short work of that business; for I'll take mine oath 'tis he.

GRIPUS - I should be glad it were.

SOSIA - How! glad it were? with your damned interrogatories, when you ought to be thankful, that so it is.

GRIPUS - [Aside.] That I may see my mistress Phædra, and present her with my great gold goblet.

SOSIA - If this be not the true Amphitryon, I wish I may be kept without doors, fasting, and biting my own fingers, for want of victuals; and that's a dreadful imprecation! I am for the inviting, and eating, and treating Amphitryon; I am sure 'tis he that is my lawfully begotten lord; and, if you had an ounce of true justice in you, you ought to have laid hold on the other Amphitryon, and committed him for a rogue, and an impostor, and a vagabond. [The Door is opened.

MERCURY - [From within.] Enter quickly, masters: The passage, on the right hand, leads to the gallery, where my lord expects you; for I am called another way.

[GRIPUS, TRANIO, and POLIDAS, go into the House.

SOSIA - I should know that voice by a secret instinct; 'tis a tongue of my family, and belongs to my brother Sosia: it must be so; for it carries a cudgelling kind of sound in it.—But put the worst: Let me weigh this matter wisely: Here's a beating, and a belly-full, against no beating, and no belly-full. The beating is bad; but the dinner is good. Now, not to be beaten, is but negatively good; but, not to fill my belly, is positively bad. Upon the whole matter, my final resolution is, to take the good and the bad as they come together.

[Is entering: MERCURY meets him at the Door.

MERCURY - Whither now, ye kitchen-scum? From whence this impudence, to enter here without permission?

SOSIA - Most illustrious sir, my ticket is my hunger: Show the full bowels of your compassion to the empty bowels of my famine.

MERCURY - Were you not charged to return no more? I'll cut you into quarters, and hang you upon the shambles.

SOSIA - You'll get but little credit by me. Alas, sir, I am but mere carrion! Brave Sosia, compassionate coward Sosia; and beat not thyself, in beating me.

MERCURY - Who gave you that privilege, sirrah, to assume my name? have you not been sufficiently warned of it, and received part of punishment already?

SOSIA - May it please you, sir, the name is big enough for both of us; and we may use it in common, like a strumpet. Witness heaven, that I would have obeyed you, and quitted my title to the name; but, wherever I come, the malicious world will call me Sosia, in spite of me. I am sensible there are two Amphitryons; and why may there not be two Sosias? Let those two cut one another's throats at their own pleasure; but you and I will be wiser, by my consent, and hold good intelligence together.

MERCURY - No, no; two Sosias would but make two fools.

SOSIA - Then let me be the fool, and be you the prudent person; and chuse for yourself some wiser name: Or you shall be the eldest brother; and I'll be content to be the younger, though I lose my inheritance.

MERCURY - I tell thee, I am the only son of our family.

SOSIA - Ah! Then let me be your bastard brother, and the son of a whore; I hope that's but reasonable.

MERCURY - No, thou shall not disgrace my father; for there are few bastards now-a-days worth owning.

SOSIA - Ah, poor Sosia! what will become of thee?

MERCURY - Yet again profanely using my proper name?

SOSIA - I did not mean myself; I was thinking of another Sosia, a poor fellow, that was once of my acquaintance, unfortunately banished out of doors, when dinner was just coming upon the table.

Enter PHAEDRA.

PHAEDRA - Sosia, you and I must—Bless me! what have we here? a couple of you? or do I see double?

SOSIA - I would fain bring it about, that I might make one of them; but he's unreasonable, and will needs incorporate me, and swallow me whole into himself. If he would be content to be but one-and-a-half, 'twould never grieve me.

MERCURY - 'Tis a perverse rascal: I kick him, and cudgel him, to no purpose; for still he's obstinate to stick to me; and I can never beat him out of my resemblance.

PHAEDRA - Which of you two is Sosia? for t'other must be the devil.

SOSIA - You had best ask him, that has played the devil with my back and sides.

MERCURY - You had best ask him,—who gave you the gold goblet?

PHAEDRA - No, that's already given; but he shall be my Sosia, that will give me such another.

MERCURY - I find you have been interloping, sirrah.

SOSIA - No, indeed, sir; I only promised her a gold thimble, which was as much as comes to my proportion of being Sosia.

PHAEDRA - This is no Sosia for my money; beat him away, t'other Sosia; he grows insufferable.

SOSIA - [Aside.] Would I were valiant, that I might beat him away; and succeed him at the dinner, for a pragmatical son of a whore, as he is!

MERCURY - What's that you are muttering betwixt your teeth, of a son of a whore, sirrah?

SOSIA - I am sure, I meant you no offence; for, if I am not Sosia, I am the son of a whore, for aught I know; and, if you are Sosia, you may be the son of a whore, for aught you know.

MERCURY - Whatever I am, I will be Sosia, as long as I please; and whenever you visit me, you shall be sure of the civility of the cudgel.

SOSIA - If you will promise to beat me into the house, you may begin when you please with me; but to be beaten out of the house, at dinner-time, flesh and blood can never bear it.

[Mercury beats him about, and Sosia is still making towards the Door; but Mercury gets betwixt, and at length drives him off the Stage.

PHAEDRA - In the name of wonder, what are you, that are Sosia, and are not Sosia?

MERCURY - If thou would'st know more of me, my person is freely at thy disposing.

PHAEDRA - Then I dispose of it to you again; for 'tis so ugly, 'tis not for my use.

MERCURY - I can be ugly, or handsome, as I please; go to bed old, and rise young. I have so many suits of persons by me, I can shift them when I will.

PHAEDRA - You are a fool, then, to put on your worst clothes, when you come a-wooing.

MERCURY - Go to; ask no more questions. I am for thy turn; for I know thy heart, and see all thou hast about thee.

PHAEDRA - Then you can see my backside too; there's a bargain for you.

MERCURY - In thy right pocket:—let me see; three love letters from judge Gripus, written to the bottom, on three sides; full of fustian passion, and hearty nonsense: as also, in the same pocket, a letter of thine intended to him, consisting of nine lines and a half, scrawled and false spelled, to show thou art a woman; and full of fraudulence, and equivocations, and shoeing-horns of love to him; to promise much, and mean nothing; to show, over and above, that thou art a mere woman.

PHAEDRA - Is the devil in you, to see all this? Now, for heaven's sake, do not look in t'other pocket.

MERCURY - Nay, there's nothing there, but a little godly prayer-book, and a bawdy lampoon, and—

PHAEDRA - [Giving a great frisk.] Look no farther, I beseech you.

MERCURY - And a silver spoon—

PHAEDRA - [Shrieking.] Ah!—

MERCURY - Which you purloined last night from Bromia.

PHAEDRA - Keep my counsel, or I am undone for ever. [Holding up her hands to him.

MERCURY - No; I'll mortify thee, now I have an handle to thy iniquity, if thou wilt not love me.

PHAEDRA - Well, if you'll promise me to be secret, I will love you; because indeed I dare do no other.

MERCURY - 'Tis a good girl; I will be secret: and, further, I will be assisting to thee in thy filching; for thou and I were born under the same planet.

PHAEDRA - And we shall come to the same end too, I'm afraid.

MERCURY - No, no; since thou hast wit enough already to cozen a judge, thou needst never fear hanging.

PHAEDRA - And will you make yourself a younger man, and be handsome too, and rich? for you, that know hearts, must needs know, that I shall never be constant to such an ugly old Sosia.

MERCURY - Thou shalt know more of that another time; in the mean while, here is a cast of my office for thee.

[He stamps upon the ground: some Dancers come from under-ground; and others from the sides of the Stage: a Song, and a fantastic Dance.

MERCURY'S SONG TO PHÆDRA.
Fair Iris, I love, and hourly I die,
But not for a lip, nor a languishing eye:
She's fickle and false, and there we agree;
For I am as false and as fickle as she.
We neither believe, what either can say;
And, neither believing, we neither betray;

'Tis civil to swear, and say things of course;
We mean not the taking for better for worse.
When present, we love; when absent, agree:
I think not of Iris, nor Iris of me:
The legend of love no couple can find,
So easy to part, or so equally joined.

After, the Dance.

PHAEDRA - This power of yours makes me suspect you for little better than a god; but if you are one, for more certainty, tell me what I am just now thinking.

MERCURY - Why, thou art thinking,—let me see; for thou art a woman, and your minds are so variable, that it is very hard, even for a god, to know them,—but, to satisfy thee, thou art wishing, now, for the same power I have exercised, that thou might'st stamp like me, and have more singers come up for another song.

PHAEDRA - Gad, I think the devil's in you. Then I do stamp in somebody's name, but I know not whose: [Stamps.] Come up, gentle-folks from below, and sing me a pastoral dialogue, where the woman may have the better of the man; as we always have in love-matters.

[New Singers come up, and sing a Song.

A PASTORAL DIALOGUE BETWIXT THYRSIS AND IRIS.
Thyrsis. Fair Iris and her swain
Were in a shady bower;
Where Thyrsis long in vain
Had sought the shepherd's hour:

At length his hand advancing upon her snowy breast;
He said, O kiss me longer,
And longer yet, and longer,
If you will make me blest

Iris. An easy yielding maid,
By trusting, is undone;
Our sex is oft betray'd,
By granting love too soon.
If you desire to gain me, your sufferings to redress,
Prepare to love me longer,
And longer yet, and longer,
Before you shall possess.

Thyrsis. The little care you show
Of all my sorrows past,
Makes death appear too slow,
And life too long to last.
Fair Iris kiss me kindly, in pity of my fate;
And kindly still, and kindly,
Before it be too late.

Iris. You fondly court your bliss,
And no advances make;
'Tis not for maids to kiss,
But 'tis for men to take.
So you may kiss me kindly, and I will not rebel;
And kindly still, and kindly,
But kiss me not and tell.

A RONDEAU.
Chorus. Thus at the height we love and live,
And fear not to be poor;
We give, and give, and give, and give,
'Till we can give no more,
But what to-day will take away,
To-morrow will restore:
Thus at the height we love, and live,
And fear not to be poor.

PHAEDRA - Adieu, I leave you to pay the music. Hope well, Mr. Planet; there is a better heaven in store for you: I say no more, but you can guess.

MERCURY - [alone.] Such bargain-loves, as I with Phædra treat,
Are all the leagues and friendships of the great;
All seek their ends, and each would other cheat.
They only seem to hate, and seem to love;
But interest is the point on which they move.
Their friends are foes, and foes are friends again,
And, in their turns, are knaves, and honest men.
Our iron age is grown an age of gold:

'Tis who bids most; for all men will be sold.

[Exit.

ACT V

SCENE I

Enter GRIPUS and PHAEDRA. GRIPUS has the Goblet in his hand.

PHAEDRA - You will not be so base to take it from me?

GRIPUS - 'Tis my proper chattel; and I'll seize my own, in whatever hands I find it.

PHAEDRA - You know I only showed it you, to provoke your generosity, that you might out-bid your rival with a better present.

GRIPUS - My rival is a thief; and I'll indite you for a receiver of stolen goods.

PHAEDRA - Thou hide-bound lover!

GRIPUS - Thou very mercenary mistress!

PHAEDRA - Thou most mercenary magistrate!

GRIPUS - Thou seller of thyself!

PHAEDRA - Thou seller of other people: thou weather-cock of government; that, when the wind blows for the subject, pointest to privilege; and when it changes for the sovereign, veerest to prerogative!

GRIPUS - Will you compound, and take it as my present?

PHAEDRA - No; but I'll send thy rival to force it from thee.

GRIPUS - When a thief is rival to his judge, the hangman will soon decide the difference.

[Exit PHAEDRA.

Enter MERCURY, with two Swords.

MERCURY - [Bowing.] Save your good lordship.

GRIPUS - From an impertinent coxcomb: I am out of humour, and am in haste; leave me.

MERCURY - 'Tis my duty to attend on your lordship, and to ease you of that undecent burden.

GRIPUS - Gold was never any burden to one of my profession.

MERCURY - By your lordship's permission, Phædra has sent me to take it from you.

GRIPUS - What, by violence?

MERCURY - [still bowing.] No; but by your honour's permission, I am to restore it to her, and persuade your lordship to renounce your pretensions to her.

GRIPUS - Tell her flatly, I will neither do one, nor t'other.

MERCURY - O my good lord, I dare pass my word for your free consent to both. Will your honour be pleased to take your choice of one of these?

GRIPUS - Why, these are swords: what have I to do with them?

MERCURY - Only to take your choice of one of them, which your lordship pleases; and leave the other to your most obedient servant.

GRIPUS - What, one of these ungodly weapons? Take notice, I'll lay you by the heels, sirrah: this has the appearance of an unlawful bloody challenge.

MERCURY - You magistrates are pleased to call it so, my lord; but with us swordmen, it is an honourable invitation to the cutting of one another's throats.

GRIPUS - Be answered; I have no throat to cut. The law shall decide our controversy.

MERCURY - By your permission, my lord, it must be dispatched this way.

GRIPUS - I'll see thee hanged before I give thee any such permission, to dispatch me into another world.

MERCURY - At the least, my lord, you have no occasion to complain of my want of respect to you. You will neither restore the goblet, nor renounce Phædra: I offer you the combat; you refuse it; all this is done in the forms of honour: It follows, that I am to affront, cudgel you, or kick you, at my own arbitrement; and, I suppose, you are too honourable not to approve of my proceeding.

GRIPUS - Here is a new sort of process, that was never heard of in any of our courts.

MERCURY - This, my good lord, is law in short-hand, without your long preambles, and tedious repetitions that signify nothing but to squeeze the subject: therefore, with your lordship's favour, I begin. [Fillips him under the chin.

GRIPUS - What is this for?

MERCURY - To give you an occasion of returning me a box o' the ear; that so all things may proceed methodically.

GRIPUS - I put in no answer, but suffer a non-suit.

MERCURY - No, my lord; for the costs and charges are to be paid: will you please to restore the cup?

GRIPUS - I told thee, no.

MERCURY - Then from your chin, I must ascend to your lordship's ears.

GRIPUS - Oh, oh, oh, oh!—Wilt thou never leave lugging me by the ears?

MERCURY - Not till your lordship will be pleased to hear reason. [Pulling again.

GRIPUS - Take the cup, and the devil give thee joy on't.

MERCURY - [Still holding him.] And your lordship will farther be graciously pleased, to release all claims, titles, and actions whatsoever, to Phædra: you must give me leave to add one small memento for that too. [Pulling him again.

GRIPUS - I renounce her; I release her.

Enter PHAEDRA.

MERCURY - [To her.] Phædra, my lord has been pleased to be very gracious, without pushing matters to extremity.

PHAEDRA - I overheard it all; but give me livery and seisin of the goblet, in the first place.

MERCURY - There is an act of oblivion should be passed too.

PHAEDRA - Let him begin to remember quarrels, when he dares; now I have him under my girdle, I'll cap verses with him to the end of the chapter.

Enter AMPHITRYON, and Guards.

AMPHITRYON - [To Gripus.] At the last I have got possession without your lordship's warrant.—Phædra, tell Alcmena I am here.

PHAEDRA - I'll carry no such lying message: you are not here, and you cannot be here; for, to my knowledge, you are above with my lady, in the chamber.

AMPHITRYON - All of a piece, and all witchcraft!—Answer me precisely: dost thou not know me for Amphitryon?

PHAEDRA - Answer me first: did you give me a diamond and a purse of gold?

AMPHITRYON - Thou knowest I did not.

PHAEDRA - Then, by the same token, I know you are not the true Amphitryon: if you are he, I am sure I left you in bed with your own wife. Now you had best stretch out a leg, and feel about for a fair lady.

AMPHITRYON - I'll undo this enchantment with my sword, and kill the sorcerer.—Come up, gentlemen, and follow me. [To the Guards.

PHAEDRA - I'll save you the labour, and call him down to confront you, if you dare attend him. [Exit Phædra.

MERCURY - [Aside.] Now the spell is ended, and Jupiter can enchant no more; or else Amphitryon had not entered so easily. [Gripus is stealing off.]—Whither now, Gripus? I have business for you: if you offer to stir, you know what follows.

Enter JUPITER, followed by TRANIO and POLIDAS.

JUPITER - Who dares to play the master in my house?
What noise is this that calls me from above,
Invades my soft recess and privacy,
And, like a tide, breaks in upon my love?

AMPHITRYON - O heavens, what's this I see?

TRANIO - What prodigy!

POLIDAS - How! two Amphitryons!

GRIPUS - I have beheld the appearance of two suns,
But still the false was dimmer than the true;
Here, both shine out alike.

AMPHITRYON - This is a sight, that, like the gorgon's head,
Runs through my limbs, and stiffens me to stone.
I need no more inquire into my fate;
For what I see resolves my doubts too plain.

TRANIO - Two drops of water cannot be more like.

POLIDAS - They are two very sames.

MERCURY - Our Jupiter is a great comedian, he counterfeits most admirably: sure his priests have copied their hypocrisy from their master. [Aside.

AMPHITRYON - Now I am gathered back into myself:
My heart beats high, and pushes out the blood, [Drawing his sword.
To give me just revenge on this impostor.
If you are brave, assist me—not one stirs! [To the Guards.
What, are all bribed to take the enchanter's part?
'Tis true, the work is mine; and thus—

[Going to rush upon Jupiter; and is held by TRANIO and POLIDAS.

POLIDAS - It must not be.

JUPITER - Give him his way; I dare the madman's worst:
But still take notice, that it looks not like
The true Amphitryon, to fly out at first
To brutal force: it shews he doubts his cause,
Who dares not trust his reason to defend it.

AMPHITRYON - Thou base usurper of my name and bed! [Struggling.
No less than thy heart's blood can wash away
The affronts I have sustained.

TRANIO - We must not suffer
So strange a duel, as Amphitryon
To fight against himself.

POLIDAS - Nor think we wrong you, when we hold your hands:
We know our duty to our general;
We know the ties of friendship to our friend;
But who that friend, or who that general is,
Without more certain proofs, betwixt you two,
Is hard to be distinguished, by our reason;
Impossible, by sight.

AMPHITRYON - I know it, and have satisfied myself;
I am the true Amphitryon.

JUPITER - See again,
He shuns the certain proofs; and dares not stand
Impartial judgment, and award of right.
But, since Alcmena's honour is concerned,
Whom, more than heaven, and all the world, I love,
This I propose, as equal to us both:—
Tranio and Polidas, be you assistants;
The guards be ready to secure the impostor,
When once so proved, for public punishment;
And Gripus, be thou umpire of the cause.

AMPHITRYON - I am content: let him proceed to examination.

GRIPUS - On whose side would you please that I should give the sentence?

[Aside to MERCURY.

MERCURY - Follow thy conscience for once; but not to make a custom of it neither, nor to leave an evil precedent of uprightness to future judges. [Aside.]—'Tis a good thing to have a magistrate under correction: your old fornicating judge dares never give sentence against him that knows his haunts.

POLIDAS - Your lordship knows I was master of Amphitryon's ship; and desire to know of him, what passed, in private, betwixt us two at his landing, when he was just ready to engage the enemy?

GRIPUS - Let the true Amphitryon answer first.

JUPITER - and AMPHITRYON - together. My lord, I told him—

GRIPUS - Peace, both of you:—'Tis a plain case they are both true; for they both speak together: but, for more certainty, let the false Amphitryon speak first.

MERCURY - Now they are both silent.

GRIPUS - Then 'tis plain, on the other side, that they are both false Amphitryons.

MERCURY - Which Amphitryon shall speak first?

GRIPUS - Let the cholerick Amphitryon speak; and let the peaceable hold his peace.

AMPHITRYON - [To POLIDAS.] You may remember that I whispered you, not to part from the stern one single moment.

POLIDAS - You did so.

GRIPUS - No more words then: I proceed to sentence.

JUPITER - 'Twas I that whispered him; and he may remember I gave him this reason for it, that, if our men were beaten, I might secure my own retreat.

POLIDAS - You did so.

GRIPUS - Now again he is as true as the other.

TRANIO - You know I was paymaster: what directions did you give me the night before the battle?

GRIPUS - To which of the you's art thou speaking?

MERCURY - It should be a double u; but they have no such letter in their tongue. [Aside.

AMPHITRYON - I ordered you to take particular care of the great bag.

GRIPUS - Why this is demonstration.

JUPITER - The bag, that I recommended to you, was of tygers-skin; and marked Beta.

GRIPUS - In sadness, I think they are both jugglers: here is nothing, and here is nothing; and then hiccius doccius, and they are both here again.

TRANIO - You peaceable Amphitryon, what money was there in that bag?

JUPITER - The sum, in gross, amounted just to fifty Attick talents.

TRANIO - To a farthing.

GRIPUS - Paugh: Obvious, obvious.

AMPHITRYON - Two thousand pieces of gold were tied up in a handkerchief, by themselves.

TRANIO - I remember it.

GRIPUS - Then it is dubious again.

JUPITER - But the rest was not all silver; for there were just four thousand brass half-pence.

GRIPUS - Being but brass, the proof is inconsiderable: if they had been silver, it had gone on your side.

AMPHITRYON - Death and hell, you will not persuade me, that I did not kill Pterelas? [To Jupiter.

JUPITER - Nor you me, that I did not enjoy Alcmena?

AMPHITRYON - That last was poison to me.— [Aside.
Yet there's one proof thou canst not counterfeit:
In killing Pterelas, I had a wound
Full in the brawny part of my right arm,
Where still the scar remains:—now blush, impostor;
For this thou canst not show.
[Bares his arm, and shows the scar, which they all look on.

OMNES - This is the true Amphitryon.

JUPITER - May your lordship please—

GRIPUS - No, sirrah, it does not please me: hold your tongue, I charge you, for the case is manifest.

JUPITER - By your favour then, this shall speak for me. [Bares his arm, and shows it.

TRANIO - 'Tis just in the same muscle.

POLIDAS - Of the same length and breadth; and the scar of the same blueish colour.

GRIPUS - [To JUPITER.] Did not I charge you not to speak? 'twas plain enough before; and now you have puzzled it again.

AMPHITRYON - Good gods, how can this be!

GRIPUS - For certain there was but one Pterelas; and he must have been in the plot against himself too; for he was killed first by one of them, and then rose again out of respect to the other Amphitryon, to be killed twice over.

Enter ALCMENA, PHAEDRA, and BROMIA.

ALCMENA - No more of this; it sounds impossible
[Turning to PHAEDRA and BROMIA.
That two should be so like, no difference found.

PHAEDRA - You'll find it true.

ALCMENA - Then where's Alcmena's honour and her fame?
Farewell my needless fear, it cannot be:
This is a case too nice for vulgar sight;
But let me come, my heart will guide my eyes
To point, and tremble to its proper choice. [Seeing Amphitryon, goes to him.
There neither was, nor is, but one Amphitryon;

And I am only his.— [Goes to take him by the hand.

AMPHITRYON - Away, adultress! [Pushing her away from him.

JUPITER - My gentle love, my treasure, and my joy,
Follow no more that false and foolish fire,
That would mislead thy fame to sure destruction!
Look on thy better husband, and thy friend,
Who will not leave thee liable to scorn,
But vindicate thy honour from that wretch,
Who would by base aspersions blot thy virtue.

ALCMENA - [Going to him, who embraces her.]
I was indeed mistaken; thou art he!
Thy words, thy thoughts, thy soul is all Amphitryon.
The impostor has thy features, not thy mind;
The face might have deceived me in my choice,
Thy kindness is a guide that cannot err.

AMPHITRYON - What! in my presence to prefer the villain?
O execrable cheat!—I break the truce;
And will no more attend your vain decisions:
To this, and to the gods, I'll trust my cause.
[Is rushing upon Jupiter, and is held again.

JUPITER - Poor man, how I contemn those idle threats!
Were I disposed, thou might'st as safely meet
The thunder launched from the red arm of Jove,—Nor
Jove need blush to be Alcmena's champion.
But in the face of Thebes she shall be cleared;
And what I am, and what thou art, be known.—
Attend, and I will bring convincing proofs.

AMPHITRYON - Thou would'st elude my justice, and escape:
But I will follow thee through earth and seas;
Nor hell shall hide thee from my just revenge.

JUPITER - I'll spare thy pains. It shall be quickly seen,
Betwixt us two, who seeks, and who avoids.—
Come in, my friends,—and thou, who seem'st Amphitryon—
That all, who are in doubt, may know the true.

[JUPITER re-enters the house; with him AMPHITRYON, ALCMENA, POLIDAS, TRANIO, and Guards.

MERCURY - Thou, Gripus, and you, Bromia, stay with Phædra:
[To Gripus and Bromia, who are following.
Let their affairs alone, and mind we ours,
Amphitryon's rival shall appear a god:
But know beforehand, I am Mercury;
Who want not heaven, while Phædra is on earth.

BROMIA - But, an't please your lordship, is my fellow Phædra to be exalted into the heavens, and made a star?

PHAEDRA - When that comes to pass, if you look up a-nights, I shall remember old kindness, and vouch-safe to twinkle on you.

Enter Sosia, peeping about him; and, seeing Mercury, is starting back.

SOSIA - Here he is again; and there's no passing by him into the house, unless I were a sprite, to glide in through the key-hole. I am to be a vagabond, I find.

MERCURY - Sosia, come back.

SOSIA - No, I thank you; you may whistle me long enough; a beaten dog has always the wit to avoid his master.

MERCURY - I permit thee to be Sosia again.

SOSIA - 'Tis an unfortunate name, and I abandon it: he that has an itch to be beaten, let him take it up for Sosia;—What have I said now! I mean for me; for I neither am nor will be Sosia.

MERCURY - But thou may'st be so in safety; for I have acknowledged myself to be god Mercury.

SOSIA - You may be a god, for aught I know; but the devil take me if ever I worship you, for an unmerciful deity as you are.

MERCURY - You ought to take it for an honour to be drubbed by the hand of a divinity.

SOSIA - I am your most humble servant, good Mr God; but, by the faith of a mortal, I could well have spared the honour that you did me. But how shall I be sure that you will never assume my shape again?

MERCURY - Because I am weary of wearing so villainous an outside.

SOSIA - Well, well; as villainous as it is, here's old Bromia will be contented with it.

BROMIA - Yes, now I am sure that I may chastise you safely, and that there's no god lurking under your appearance.

SOSIA - Ay; but you had best take heed how you attempt it; for, as Mercury has turned himself into me, so I may take the toy into my head, and turn myself into Mercury, that I may swinge you off condignly.

MERCURY - In the mean time, be all my witnesses, that I take Phædra for my wife of the left hand; that is, in the nature of a lawful concubine.

PHAEDRA - You shall pardon me for believing you, for all you are a god; for you have a terrible ill name below; and I am afraid you'll get a footman, instead of a priest, to marry us.

MERCURY - But here's Gripus shall draw up articles betwixt us.

PHAEDRA - But he's damnably used to false conveyancing. Well, be it so; for my counsel shall overlook them before I sign—Come on, Gripus, that I may have him under black and white.

[Here GRIPUS gets ready pen, ink, and paper.

MERCURY - With all my heart, that I may have thee under black and white hereafter.

PHAEDRA - [To Gripus.] Begin, begin—Heads of articles to be made, &c. betwixt Mercury, god of thieves—

MERCURY - And Phædra, queen of gypsies.—Imprimis, I promise to buy and settle upon her an estate, containing nine thousand acres of land, in any part of Bœotia, to her own liking.

PHAEDRA - Provided always, that no part of the said nine thousand acres shall be upon, or adjoining to, Mount Parnassus; for I will not be fobbed off with a poetical estate.

MERCURY - Memorandum, that she be always constant to me, and admit of no other lover.

PHAEDRA - Memorandum, unless it be a lover that offers more; and that the constancy shall not exceed the settlement.

MERCURY - Item, that she shall keep no male servants in her house: Item, no rival lap-dog for a bedfellow: Item, that she shall never pray to any of the gods.

PHAEDRA - What, would you have me an atheist?

MERCURY - No devotion to any he-deity, good Phædra.

BROMIA - Here's no provision made for children yet.

PHAEDRA - Well remembered, Bromia; I bargain that my eldest son shall be a hero, and my eldest daughter a king's mistress.

MERCURY - That is to say, a blockhead, and a harlot, Phædra.

PHAEDRA - That's true; but who dares call them so? Then, for the younger children—But now I think on't, we'll have no more, but Mass and Miss; for the rest would be but chargeable, and a burden to the nation.

MERCURY - Yes, yes; the second shall be a false prophet: he shall have wit enough to set up a new religion, and too much wit to die a martyr for it.

PHAEDRA - O what had I forgot? there's pin-money, and alimony, and separate maintenance, and a thousand things more to be considered, that are all to be tacked to this act of settlement.

SOSIA - I am a fool, I must confess; but yet I can see as far into a mill-stone as the best of you. I have observed, that you women-wits are commonly so quick upon the scent, that you often over-run it: now I would ask of Madam Phædra, that in case Mr Heaven there should be pleased to break these articles, in what court of judicature she intends to sue him?

PHAEDRA - The fool has hit upon't:—Gods, and great men, are never to be sued, for they can always plead privilege of peerage; and therefore for once, monsieur, I'll take your word; for, as long as you love me, you'll be sure to keep it: and, in the mean time, I shall be gaining experience how to manage some rich cully; for no woman ever made her fortune by a wit.

It thunders; and the company within doors, Amphitryon, Alcmena, Polidas, and Tranio, all come running out, and join with the rest, who were on the stage before.

AMPHITRYON - Sure 'tis some god; he vanished from our sight,
And told us, we should see him soon return.

ALCMENA - I know not what to hope, nor what to fear.
A simple error is a real crime,
And unconsenting innocence is lost.

A second peal of Thunder. After which, JUPITER appears in a Machine.

JUPITER - Look up, Amphitryon, and behold, above,
The impostor god, the rival of thy love;
In thy own shape see Jupiter appear,
And let that sight secure thy jealous fear.
Disgrace, and infamy, are turned to boast;
No fame, in Jove's concurrence, can be lost:
What he enjoys, he sanctifies from vice,
And, by partaking, stamps into a price,
'Tis I who ought to murmur at my fate,
Forced by my love my godhead to translate;
When on no other terms I could possess,
But by thy form, thy features, and thy dress.
To thee were given the blessings that I sought,
Which else, not all the bribes of heaven had bought,
Then take into thy arms thy envied love,
And, in his own despite, triumph o'er Jove.

MERCURY, AMPHITRYON and ALCMENA both stand mute, and know not how to take it. [Aside.

SOSIA - Our sovereign lord Jupiter is a sly companion; he knows how to gild a bitter pill. [Aside.

JUPITER - From this auspicious night shall rise an heir,
Great like his sire, and like his mother fair:
Wrongs to redress, and tyrants to disseize;
Born for a world that wants a Hercules.
Monsters, and monster-men he shall engage,
And toil, and struggle, through an impious age.

Peace to his labours shall at length succeed;
And murmuring men, unwilling to be freed,
Shall be compelled to happiness, by need.
[Jupiter is carried back to Heaven.

OMNES - We all congratulate Amphitryon.

MERCURY - Keep your congratulations to yourselves, gentlemen. 'Tis a nice point, let me tell you that; and the less that's said of it the better. Upon the whole matter, if Amphitryon takes the favour of Jupiter in patience, as from a god, he's a good heathen.

SOSIA - I must take a little extraordinary pains to-night, that my spouse may come even with her lady, and produce a squire to attend on young Hercules, when he goes out to seek adventures; that, when his master kills a man, he may stand ready to pick his pockets, and piously relieve his aged parents.—Ah, Bromia, Bromia, if thou hadst been as handsome and as young as Phædra!—I say no more, but somebody might have made his fortunes as well as his master, and never the worse man neither.

For, let the wicked world say what they please,
The fair wife makes her husband live at ease:
The lover keeps him too; and but receives,
Like Jove, the remnants that Amphitryon leaves.
'Tis true, the lady has enough in store,
To satisfy those two, and eke two more:
In fine, the man, who weighs the matter fully,
Would rather be the cuckold than the cully.

[Exeunt.

EPILOGUE

SPOKEN BY PHÆDRA

I'm thinking, (and it almost makes me mad)
How sweet a time those heathen ladies had.
Idolatry was even their Gods' own trade:
They worshipped the fine creatures they had made.
Cupid was chief of all the deities;
And love was all the fashion, in the skies.
When the sweet nymph held up the lily hand,
Jove was her humble servant at command;
The treasury of heaven was ne'er so bare,
But still there was a pension for the fair.
In all his reign, adultery was no sin;
For Jove the good example did begin.
Mark, too, when he usurped the husband's name,
How civilly he saved the lady's fame.
The secret joys of love he wisely hid;
But you, sirs, boast of more than e'er you did.
You teaze your cuckolds, to their face torment 'em;
But Jove gave his new honours to content him,
And, in the kind remembrance of the fair,
On each exalted son bestowed a star.
For these good deeds, as by the date appears,
His godship flourished full two thousand years.

At last, when he and all his priests grew old,
The ladies grew in their devotion cold;
And that false worship would no longer hold.
Severity of life did next begin;
And always does, when we no more can sin.
That doctrine, too, so hard in practice lies,
That the next age may see another rise.

Then, pagan gods may once again succeed:
And Jove, or Mars, be ready, at our need,
To get young godlings; and so mend our breed.

John Dryden – A Short Biography

John Dryden was born on August 9th, 1631 in the village rectory of Aldwincle near Thrapston in Northamptonshire, where his maternal grandfather was Rector of All Saints Church.

Dryden was the eldest of fourteen children born to Erasmus Dryden and wife Mary Pickering, paternal grandson of Sir Erasmus Dryden, 1st Baronet (1553–1632) and wife Frances Wilkes, Puritan landowning gentry who supported the Puritan cause and Parliament.

As a boy Dryden lived in the nearby village of Titchmarsh, Northamptonshire where it is probable that he received his first education.

In 1644 he was sent to Westminster School as a King's Scholar where his headmaster was Dr. Richard Busby, a charismatic teacher but severe disciplinarian. Having recently been re-founded by Elizabeth I, Westminster now embraced a very different religious and political spirit encouraging royalism and high Anglicanism but as a humanist public school, it maintained a curriculum which trained pupils in the art of rhetoric and the presentation of arguments for both sides of a given issue. This skill would remain with Dryden and influence his later writing and thinking, as much of it displays these dialectical patterns.

His first published poem, whilst still at Westminster, was an elegy with a strong royalist flavour on the death of his schoolmate Henry, Lord Hastings from smallpox, and alludes to the execution of King Charles I, which took place on January 30th, 1649.

In 1650 Dryden was ready for University and travelled to Trinity College, Cambridge. Dryden's undergraduate years would almost certainly have followed the standard curriculum of classics, rhetoric, and mathematics.

Dryden obtained his BA in 1654, graduating top of the list for Trinity that year.

However family tragedy struck in June of the same year when Dryden's father died, leaving him some land which generated a small income, but not enough to live on.

Returning to London during The Protectorate, Dryden now obtained work with Cromwell's Secretary of State, John Thurloe. This may have been the result of influence exercised on his behalf by his cousin the Lord Chamberlain, Sir Gilbert Pickering.

At Cromwell's funeral on 23 November 1658 Dryden was in the company of the Puritan poets John Milton and Andrew Marvell. The setting was to be a sea change in English history. From Republic to Monarchy and from one set of lauded poets to what would soon become the Age of Dryden.

The start began later that year when Dryden published the first of his great poems, Heroic Stanzas (1658), a eulogy on Cromwell's death which is necessarily cautious and prudent in its emotional display.

With the Restoration of the Monarchy in 1660 Dryden celebrated in verse with Astraea Redux, an authentic royalist panegyric. In this work the interregnum is illustrated as a time of anarchy, and Charles is seen as the restorer of peace and order.

With the king now established Dryden moved quickly to place himself as the leading poet and critic of his day and transferred his allegiances to the new government.

Along with Astraea Redux, Dryden welcomed the new regime with two more panegyrics: To His Sacred Majesty: A Panegyric on his Coronation (1662) and To My Lord Chancellor (1662).

These panegyrics are occasional and written to celebrate events. Thus they are written for the nation rather than the self, but these and others put him in good standing for his eventual appointment as Poet Laureate, where a number of event poems would be required each year and speaking for the Nation and to the Nation would be the first order of duty.

These poems suggest that Dryden was looking to court a possible patron which would have given him an income and time to explore his creative ideas but no, his path instead would be to make a living in writing for publishers, not for the aristocracy, and thus ultimately for the reading public.

In November 1662 Dryden was proposed for membership in the Royal Society, and he was elected an early fellow. However, his inactivity and non payment of dues led to his expulsion in 1666.

On December 1st, 1663 Dryden married the Royalist sister of Sir Robert Howard—Lady Elizabeth Howard (died 1714). The marriage was at St. Swithin's, London, and the consent of the parents is noted on the license, though Lady Elizabeth was then about twenty-five. She was the object of some scandals, well or ill founded; it was said that Dryden had been bullied into the marriage by her brothers. A small estate in Wiltshire was settled upon them by her father. The lady's intellect and temper were apparently not good; her husband was treated as an inferior by those of her social status.

Dryden's works occasionally contain outbursts against the married state but also celebrations of the same. Little else is known of the intimate side of his marriage.

Both Dryden and his wife were warmly attached to their children. They had three sons: Charles (1666–1704), John (1668–1701), and Erasmus Henry (1669–1710). Lady Elizabeth Dryden survived her husband, but went insane soon after his death and died in 1714.

With the re-opening of the theatres after the Puritan ban, Dryden began to also write plays. His first play, The Wild Gallant, appeared in 1663 but was not successful. From 1668 on he was contracted to produce three plays a year for the King's Company, in which he became a shareholder. During the 1660s and '70s, theatrical writing was his main source of income. He led the way in Restoration comedy, his best-known works being Marriage à la Mode (1672), as well as heroic tragedy and regular tragedy, in which his greatest success was All for Love (1678). Dryden was never fully satisfied with his theatrical writings and frequently suggested that his talents were wasted on unworthy audiences.

Certainly therefore fame as a poet looked more rewarding. In 1667, around the same time his dramatic career began, he published Annus Mirabilis, a lengthy historical poem which described the English defeat of the Dutch naval fleet and the Great Fire of London in 1666. It was a modern epic in pentameter quatrains that established him as the pre-eminent poet of his generation, and was crucial in his attaining the posts of Poet Laureate (1668) and then historiographer royal (1670).

When the Great Plague of London closed the theatres in 1665 Dryden retreated to Wiltshire where he wrote Of Dramatick Poesie (1668), arguably the best of his unsystematic prefaces and essays. Dryden constantly defended his own literary practice, and Of Dramatick Poesie, the longest of his critical works, takes the form of a dialogue in which four characters—each based on a prominent contemporary, with Dryden himself as 'Neander'—debate the merits of classical, French and English drama.

He felt strongly about the relation of the poet to tradition and the creative process, and his heroic play Aureng-zebe (1675) has a prologue which denounces the use of rhyme in serious drama. His play All for Love (1678) was written in blank verse, and was to immediately follow Aureng-Zebe.

On December 18th, 1679 he was attacked in Rose Alley near his home in Covent Garden by thugs hired by fellow poet, John Wilmot, 2nd Earl of Rochester, with whom he had a long-standing conflict. Wilmot was constantly in and out of favour with the King and his own poetry was often bawdy, lewd, even obscene and made fun of the King who would often exile him from Court.

Dryden's greatest achievements were in satiric verse: the mock-heroic Mac Flecknoe, a more personal product of his Laureate years, was a lampoon circulated in manuscript and an attack on the playwright Thomas Shadwell. Dryden's main goal in the work is to "satirize Shadwell, ostensibly for his offenses against literature but more immediately we may suppose for his habitual badgering of him on the stage and in print." It is not a belittling form of satire, but rather one which makes his object great in ways which are unexpected, transferring the ridiculous into poetry. This line of satire continued with Absalom and Achitophel (1681) and The Medal (1682). Other major works from this period are the religious poems Religio Laici (1682), written from the position of a member of the Church of England; his 1683 edition of Plutarch's Lives, translated From the Greek by Several Hands in which he introduced the word biography to English readers; and The Hind and the Panther, (1687) which celebrates his conversion to Roman Catholicism.

He wrote Britannia Rediviva celebrating the birth of a son and heir to the Catholic King and Queen on June 10th, 1688. When later in the same year James II was deposed in the Glorious Revolution, Dryden's refusal to take the oaths of allegiance to the new monarchs, William and Mary, which left him out of favour at court and he had to leave his post as Poet Laureate. Thomas Shadwell, his despised rival, succeeded him. Dryden, England's greatest literary figure, was now forced to give up his public offices and live by the proceeds of his pen alone.

Dryden was an excellent translator with his own style which brought the ire of many critics. Many felt he would embellish or expand anything he felt short or curt. Dryden did not feel such expansion was a fault, arguing that as Latin is a naturally concise language it cannot be duly represented by a comparable number of words in the much larger English vocabulary. He continued with his task of translating works by Horace, Juvenal, Ovid, Lucretius, and Theocritus, a task which he found far more satisfying than writing for the stage.

In 1694 he began work on what would be his most ambitious and defining work as translator, The Works of Virgil (1697), which was published by subscription. The publication of the translation of Virgil was a national event and brought Dryden the sum of £1,400.

His final translations appeared in the volume Fables Ancient and Modern (1700), a series of episodes from Homer, Ovid, and Boccaccio, as well as modernised adaptations from Geoffrey Chaucer interspersed with Dryden's own poems. As a translator, he made great literary works in the older languages available to readers of English.

John Dryden died on May 12th, 1700, and was initially buried in St. Anne's cemetery in Soho, before being exhumed and reburied in Westminster Abbey ten days later. He was the subject of poetic eulogies, such as Luctus Brittannici: or the Tears of the British Muses; for the Death of John Dryden, Esq. (London, 1700), and The Nine Muses.

He is seen as dominating the literary life of Restoration England to such a point that the period came to be known in literary circles as the Age of Dryden. Walter Scott called him "Glorious John."

Dryden was the dominant literary figure and influence of his age. He established the heroic couplet as a standard form of English poetry by writing successful satires, religious pieces, fables, epigrams, compliments, prologues, and plays with it; he also introduced the alexandrine and triplet into the form. In his poems, translations, and criticism, he established a poetic diction appropriate to the heroic couplet—Auden referred to him as "the master of the middle style"—that was a model for his contemporaries and for much of the 18th century. The considerable loss felt by the English literary community at his death was evident in the elegies written about him. Dryden's heroic couplet went on to become the dominant poetic form of the 18th century.

What Dryden achieved in his poetry was neither the emotional excitement of the early nineteenth-century romantics nor the intellectual complexities of the metaphysicals. Although he uses formal structures such as heroic couplets, he tried to recreate the natural rhythm of speech, and he knew that different subjects need different kinds of verse. In his preface to Religio Laici he says that "the expressions of a poem designed purely for instruction ought to be plain and natural, yet majestic... The florid, elevated and figurative way is for the passions; for (these) are begotten in the soul by showing the objects out of their true proportion.... A man is to be cheated into passion, but to be reasoned into truth."

Perhaps the following illustrates Dryden and his life—"The way I have taken, is not so streight as Metaphrase, nor so loose as Paraphrase: Some things too I have omitted, and sometimes added of my own. Yet the omissions I hope, are but of Circumstances, and such as wou'd have no grace in English; and the Addition, I also hope, are easily deduc'd from Virgil's Sense. They will seem (at least I have the Vanity to think so), not struck into him, but growing out of him".

John Dryden – A Concise Bibliography

Astraea Redux, 1660
The Wild Gallant (comedy), 1663
The Indian Emperour (tragedy), 1665
Annus Mirabilis (poem), 1667
The Enchanted Island (comedy), 1667, with William D'Avenant from Shakespeare's The Tempest

Secret Love, or The Maiden Queen, 1667
An Essay of Dramatick Poesie, 1668
An Evening's Love (comedy), 1668
Tyrannick Love (tragedy), 1669
The Conquest of Granada, 1670
The Assignation, or Love in a Nunnery, 1672
Marriage à la mode, 1672
Amboyna, or the Cruelties of the Dutch to the English Merchants, 1673
The Mistaken Husband (comedy), 1674
Aureng-zebe, 1675
All for Love, 1678
Oedipus (heroic drama), 1679, an adaptation with Nathaniel Lee of Sophocles' Oedipus
Absalom and Achitophel, 1681
The Spanish Fryar, 1681
Mac Flecknoe, 1682
The Medal, 1682
Religio Laici, 1682
To the Memory of Mr. Oldham, 1684
Threnodia Augustalis, 1685
The Hind and the Panther, 1687
A Song for St. Cecilia's Day, 1687
Britannia Rediviva, 1688, written to mark the birth of a Prince of Wales.
Amphitryon, 1690
Don Sebastian (play), 1690
Creator Spirit, by whose aid, 1690. Translation of Rabanus Maurus' Veni Creator Spiritus
King Arthur, 1691
Cleomenes, 1692
The Art of Satire, 1693
Love Triumphant, 1694
The Works of Virgil, 1697
Alexander's Feast, 1697
Fables, Ancient and Modern, 1700

www.ingramcontent.com/pod-product-compliance
Lightning Source LLC
Chambersburg PA
CBHW071410040426
42444CB00009B/2191